Talks too much!

A candid tale of an adult
ADHD diagnosis: The good,
the bad and the chaotic

ALANA REEVES

Editing and design by Claire McGregor,
Kookaburra Hill Publishing Services

This book is dedicated to Pook,
Boris 1 and Boris 2. And also to me,
because I can't quite believe I
actually wrote a book.

The ADHD diagnosis is life-changing for adults. To discover you've spent your whole life wrestling this invisible opponent. You had no idea what was sabotaging you, or even that it's been there, undermining you your whole life, 24-7... You just assumed life is this hard for everyone.

— Rick Green CM OOnt BSc

Acknowledgements

I want to thank my husband, Neil, for keeping me sane and for being eternally patient with your neurodiverse family. For telling me to go for it when I decided to write a book. And any other ideas I come up with too, to be honest. You never question if I can do something, and this gives me the confidence to go for it. And you laugh at my jokes, so that's pretty good. You probably won't read this book and that is the 3,467th reason I love you.

To my children, for allowing me to fumble through this parenting gig and keeping me firmly in life with your endless sport, fights and moments of pure perfection. I know it was weird when I wanted to do something for myself and had to spend time on this book. I would like to say that you were both patient and understanding but that would be a lie, so I'll just say thank you for not burning the house down. Without my little guy being diagnosed, I never would have ended up on my own journey, so thank you for living very firmly outside the box. And to my big boy, thank you for being exactly who you are.

To my parents for your endless belief in me and what I can achieve. I think the fact that we had no idea that I had ADHD until now was in part because you always accepted me exactly as I am. You are my biggest champions and you make showing up as myself an easy thing to do. Knowing there are two people who are on your side no matter what does something pretty wonderful to a person. I'm so grateful that the stork delivered me to you.

Thanks to my Honey, for always holding space for me.

To Leonie, you know who you are for me.

To Kelsey, for always getting it.

To Claire, my editor, book designer, advisor and general legend. You got me straight away and gave me the encouragement I needed to go for it. Thank you for editing my book in a way that polished it but, ultimately, kept it the same. There is an art to that.

Contents

QR codes

You will see a QR code at the start of each chapter. This is my ADHD-friendly hack – simply scan the code with your phone camera and the link will take you to a page on my website where a video of me summarises the chapter.

Introduction

Welcome to the journey of my ADHD discovery and the subsequent adventure. You may have picked up this book because you've been diagnosed with ADHD. You may suspect you have ADHD. You may love someone with ADHD. You may have picked this up accidentally and thought it was a book about your ABCDs. It's not, but you may as well stay and read it now you're here.

When I first started to suspect that I had ADHD, at the tender age of 39, I began looking for books about the experience of being diagnosed as an adult woman. There was no shortage of ADHD books, but I quickly noticed a theme – they were all self-help books. Don't get me wrong, there is a time and place for self-help books. Many a self-help book has been half read by me, don't you worry about that!

But where were the raw, unfiltered stories? The ones that didn't have all the answers? I love a solution as much as the next person, but I don't view ADHD as a problem that needs to be fixed. Sure, some of us may need the help of medication (oh, man, did I find out that I needed the help of medication), therapy and accommodations, but what if instead of trying to push back against our differences, we lean into them? Just sink into the deliciousness

1

that is our creativity, our compassion and our unique differences. What about we give ourselves a *break*?

> 📝 *It is important to me to shine a light on women who are diagnosed with ADHD.* 📝

There was only one thing for it: write the book that I wanted to read. I sat down and the words just flowed out of me. I couldn't have stopped them if I'd tried. Which I didn't because I was using writing as a reason to avoid doing the dishes. I wanted to write a book that was filled with information about how ADHD *feels*. Particularly, how it feels when you're an adult who until that point had not one single clue that you had ADHD. I wanted to bring awareness to how women often cruise through life until events overpower them and their coping skills no longer cut it.

I started writing before I was officially diagnosed, and finished post-diagnosis. I started writing even though my mate, Impostor Syndrome, was telling me I shouldn't. I am so glad I ignored him. Doing it this way meant I captured exactly how it felt to be an undiagnosed, unmedicated woman who had spent her whole adult life feeling weird and uncomfortable. Things have changed immensely since then, and I don't know if I would be able to word it as well if I wrote it now.

I hope that within the pages of this book I have created a space where my imperfect and flawed self allows room for you to be your own imperfect and flawed self. It is important to me to shine a light on women who are diagnosed with ADHD, particularly women who are diagnosed later in life, like me. Those of us who have spent our lives unaware of what is "wrong" with us. Why we feel utterly overwhelmed and anxiety-ridden. Why we don't do things the same as other people. Women who have been told you're too much, too loud, too much energy, *shhhh!*, wait your turn, stop being so opinionated.

ADHD looks different for everyone, so while you may be able to relate to my story in some ways, your experiences may also be different. I have written this from my perspective, but it's important to know that even if you don't relate to everything I've been through, someone will have, so you're not alone.

You are fabulous just the way you are. I don't care that you forgot to meet me for coffee. I don't mind that you interrupt me mid-conversation to point out a funny bird. I couldn't give two hoots if you have 48 dishes in your sink and you forgot to brush your teeth for 3 days. Life isn't about trying to be like everyone else. How you are is just how I like you.

Talks too much!

Doesn't everyone feel like that?

My second son arrived in the world the way he does everything – like a bull at a gate. I had been induced at 38 weeks due to suffering from cholestasis and was enjoying being hooked up to the sweet, sweet joy that is an epidural. The labour was progressing nicely, I thought, and the midwife agreed as she had rebelled against the doctor's wishes that we hurry things up by increasing the syntocinon.

I love midwives. She bald-faced lied to the doctor that she was going to up the dose while looking him straight in the eye, then, as soon as he left, she turned to me and said, "Not bloody likely."

Anyway, things had felt a little weird "down there", so I mentioned this to her. Although, to be honest, my poor flaps had been swollen and blue (yes, blue, like hello, what the hell?) for months, so nothing had felt normal for a while. She had a quick look, gasped and said, "He's there! The baby is right there! Don't push! Stop pushing!"

Mate, I wasn't pushing. However, 5 years earlier I had pushed a 9lbs 3oz (4.16kg) baby out of there, so perhaps that had paved the way. This time, when I was allowed to push, I gave a half-hearted "Nughhh" and out he slid. Like a fish. Literally flew into the world. And into my head popped the phrase, "He's trouble."

Now, I must explain this before people start thinking I'm horrible. I did not mean this in a negative way. I have spent my life liking and being drawn to the troublemakers. I have been a troublemaker my whole life. His dad is one of the biggest troublemakers I know. And I now had two kids with the guy. So, let me clarify that when that phrase popped into my head, I was pleased as punch by it.

Right from the start he was different from his brother. He tested my boundaries like nothing else. His big brother had slept through the night when he was only one week old. His brother had breastfed until he was 14 months old. Now I had this powerhouse pocket rocket who simply would not be tamed. He would sleep through one night, and then be up for 3 hours the next. He was walking by the time he was 9 months old, running at 11 months, and jumping off small walls by the time he was 13 months. He was a firecracker. He rode a bike without training wheels just before he was 3. Just got on it and rode off. Yeah okay, don't worry about me, buddy – I'll just be over here being ROBBED of the chance to teach you how to ride a bike!

One memory that sticks out so clearly was us sitting down for a sweet, calm breastfeed. You know, we would be bathed in a beautiful calm light, with soothing music, and my son and I would be at one while he suckled on my teat. (Side note: I am fully aware I did not need to use that word – it's not even anatomically correct – but it popped into my head and made me laugh, so it stays.) Anyway, there we were... Joke!

Never happened like that. My little guy didn't want to sit and breastfeed. He wanted to run around breaking things. One time, when he was about 10 months, and I was trying to persevere with the breastfeeding, he was craning his neck around on a 180-degree angle, arching his back and generally resisting the feed. I found myself desperately clutching my own boob and sort of wobbling it in the direction of his completely closed mouth while he tried to get away from me. Like, a full fist of breast, grasped tightly and being shaken at him. Enticing, right? Which child, who categorically does not want to be breast-fed, wouldn't be motivated by having a tit literally shoved into their face? Suddenly, I had one of those moments of clarity. What the hell am I doing?

Just one of many experiences in my life where I was trying to get my oblong peg to fit into the square hole, and this child was not having it. It was the bottle life for him, and I got my boobs back.

When I look back now, it was so obvious that he had ADHD, but I had absolutely no experience with it so I didn't recognise the signs. I just accepted that he was my crazy little coconut and that was that.

It's funny how I just understood him though. I remember taking him to a new school in Year 1 and feeling like I had to pre-empt him to his teacher. Also taking him to a new after-school care place and doing the same thing. I remember saying, "He can be quite loud and active, but he has the kindest heart. Can you please look past his volume and activity levels and see who he is inside?"

I had this instinct that I needed people to see past the surface and see what was inside. I didn't want people judging him on first appearances and missing all his beautiful points. And so began a turn of events that I never saw coming.

We were a few weeks into the first term of his new school. His amazing teacher pulled me aside to discuss his behaviour. She mentioned that he was finding it hard to sit still in class.

So what? I thought. *He's 6.*

That he kept yelling out in class. I mean, he was funny, but it was distracting.

And the problem is? I thought, my mind scooting over distant memories of my own school report cards saying much the same thing.

Then that he was far behind in his work compared to the other kids. Oh, okay. You've got my attention. This was news to me. I hadn't heard any complaints from the teacher at his last school. BUT, I'm also not the parent who compares their kid to other children. They all develop in their own time. I was prepared to justify that one away too.

Then she did something weird. As part of the conversation, she mentioned that her son had ADHD.

Okay, cool story, lady, but what does that have to do with me? I thought.

Let's be honest, my face probably said it too. She kindly and gently suggested I read a book called *Understanding ADHD* by Dr Christopher Green.

Huh? Why would I read that? What a strange suggestion! I was genuinely puzzled. The denial was real in this one, my friend.

I struggled with this suggestion about my little man. Okay, so he was an absolute nutter (again, complete term of endearment), but he was funny and sparky and a BOY. It seemed to be such a jump from that to ADHD.

I'll admit that at this stage my understanding of ADHD was incredibly limited. This, combined with my rejection of "being told what to do" (I know, even I'm rolling my eyes at the ignorance), meant that I discounted it on the spot. I was *not* putting a label on my son. Nuh-uh. Which is ridiculous being that when my elder son was in Year 4, he was diagnosed with auditory processing disorder (APD). I wasn't scared of labels, but I think I feared the ADHD label. The one that really I knew nothing about apart from the generalisation of a young boy jumping around the classroom, calling out and being silly. Oh yeah, that.

> **" *I couldn't help but blame myself.*
> *What had I done wrong?* "**

When your child is diagnosed with something, although it's a relief to understand why they are having the difficulties they are, you still feel sadness for them. At the time of my elder son's diagnosis with APD, I felt awful that it had taken me so long to realise he was struggling. He was my only child for 5 years, so I had nothing to compare him to. I loved him unconditionally, and I thought he was perfect just the way he was. And he is perfect still, but he needed help as he couldn't learn in the same way that others were. I threw myself into learning about it and got him help from a fabulous speech therapist.

Fast forward 2 years, and now it was being suggested that my other guy possibly had ADHD. I drove to work bawling my eyes out and generally feeling sorry for myself and for my boys. I didn't want it to be true. I couldn't help but blame myself. What had I done wrong? It's important for me right now to emphasise that *I had done nothing wrong*. Just like if you also have children with special needs, it's not your fault either. But I want to capture how

9

I was feeling. This book, after all, is designed to make you feel like what you're feeling is normal. It's a process.

So, there I was, driving to work, bawling my eyes out.

I think it's so important to let yourself have this mourning period. For yourself, for your children. A diagnosis is one thing, but even at the start when you may be exploring the possibility of something like this, it's big, and it can be life-altering. Giving yourself time to adjust and absorb is imperative. Be kind to yourself as you navigate this brand-new world. I'm eternally grateful that I have an intrinsic streak of optimism that runs through me, so I bit the bullet, followed the teacher's advice and bought the book.

First of all: mind blown.

Second of all: distant little voice in the back of my mind that I went on to ignore for a further 12 months, *Wait... doesn't everyone feel like this*?

And then there were kids

For many people who are diagnosed with ADHD as an adult, it can seemingly come out of nowhere. For women, it can be an even bigger shock because many of us achieve academic success or breeze through school with relative ease. Being that the representation of ADHD we've become accustomed to is an image of a hyperactive little boy who won't sit still to learn and who is falling behind in class, it's hard to reconcile that with yourself, often a successful and accomplished woman. On the surface that is. Below the façade lies the secret.

I breezed through the education system, doing my homework willingly and often being recognised for my achievements. I was talented in sport, setting many school records. I played in multiple teams, for my school and for clubs. I excelled in English, drama and art, but I found all subjects easily within my scope of ability. I never scored below a B grade. I grew accustomed to the comments from teachers about my distractibility (as well as my talent for being the distracter), but as I was simultaneously chalking up academically, there wasn't much weight behind the observations. At the end of primary school, on the cusp of moving to high school, I was awarded a scholarship for being an all-round high achiever over academia, sport and behaviour. #humblebrag.

Doesn't sound like your typical kid with ADHD, does it? It wasn't until I started to suspect ADHD as an adult that I looked back on my childhood and could see some tell-tale signs. Only then was it clear that the remarks on my reports about my exuberant insistence on maintaining a constant level of chatter took on a different meaning.

After finishing Year 12, I went to work full-time. Thus began a career of finding ways to entertain myself at work. I often worked in positions in which there was room for tomfoolery. One job was as a receptionist with the distributors of a clothing brand. My boss was a woman called Kylie, who was quite young for the seniority of her position. And, of course, given my propensity for being a bit naughty, I was well up for any shenanigans she suggested.

Most notable was the time we superglued a $2 coin on the ground outside our offices. Our windows were mirrored so we could see out, but people couldn't see in. We had a whale of a time, laughing our heads off as people stopped to pick up the coin and discovered they couldn't. Until one day, when it all changed.

A tiny, bent-over elderly lady shuffled past. She must have been in her 90s. Both of us looked at each other with wide eyes, silently hoping she would have bad eyesight and not see the coin. But she did, and we looked on in horror when she began her descent down, bending painfully at the waist. It seemed to take *years* for her to get to the ground, and then she scratched at the coin with her gnarled hands. The horror! As soon as she shuffled off, we sped out of there, kicking at it with our shoes to dislodge it, with no luck. By the time we returned the next day, someone had managed to get it off. I like to think she came back with a hammer and chisel in the night. We'll never know.

Perhaps this is a little bit indicative, but after finishing school I didn't consider further study for one single moment. I couldn't bear the thought of knuckling down for more schoolwork. I had no idea what I wanted to do either, so it seemed ill-advised to study something just for the sake of it. I had always been independent, and I wanted to make my own cash.

After a few years of reception work, I started working in childcare. It appealed to me based heavily on the fact that I could be silly and hang out with kids all day. Eventually, I signed up for my Certificate III in Community Services (Children's Services). I found the study easy because it was a subject I was quite passionate about, although of course I deployed my questionable studying tactic of leaving assignments until the last minute.

Putting a few more years of work behind me, I reached the point where I decided that gallivanting overseas was my next step. Off I went, backpack on, and clutched in my hand was a passport with a working visa attached. I landed in London and promptly moved in with my friend Ange, who had grown up around the corner from me in Flagstaff Hill, Adelaide. We'd been friends since we were 5 years old and would run around the athletics field together in little yellow sports undies and a cack green t-shirt. Sports in the '80s were weird. Anyway, in Acton, London, I moved in with her and 3 to 4 thousand other Aussies.

I scored myself some nannying jobs, working for various families, which suited me to a tee because it provided the variety I craved. I was developing a history of having jobs that were only ever short term, and my dwindling interest would pull me in the direction of another bright and shiny role. It was while in London I met the man who would eventually become the father of my children.

Soon, a decade had passed since I'd finished school, and there was still not even the slightest notion that made me suspect I had ADHD. I was able to find jobs easily, I excelled in the workplace, and generally I felt like I was achieving everything I wanted to. I had meaningful relationships with people around me and didn't find it hard to behave acceptably in (most) situations. Okay, so I was not the person to look to if there was a serious conversation to be had because I would most definitely laugh, but I just put that down to a sparkling sense of humour and an innate desire to enjoy myself.

Then started a chain of events that spanned the next 12 years until I finally suspected, and was diagnosed with, ADHD.

But, we need a little more backstory to get to that point.

After I met my (future) boys' dad in London, we travelled around for a few years and then settled in his hometown of Perth, Western Australia. It was a 4-hour flight from my hometown of Adelaide, South Australia, where my family lived, and where I had grown up. In my last year at high school I did my final art project on photography, so with that in mind I scored myself a job as a school photographer. Clearly, it wasn't creative, but I quickly moved up the ranks anyway, earning myself trips to other states in Australia to photograph kids there too.

Apparently, photo day at the schools was a chance for the teachers to duck behind the bike sheds to have a smoke. I'm assuming that was what they were doing, anyway. In any case, they made the most of having some-one else to watch the kids, and they were out of there. As a result, the kids were feral. I was 25 years old. I did not DO teenagers. And I like to wear my feelings on my face. I overheard one of the kids make the iconic comment, "Why does that lady look so angry?" How dare they. I wasn't angry; I was downright filthy. I was annoyed because they were annoying. End of.

About a year into the role, I decided it was time to try for a baby. My job required a lot of heavy lifting, carrying the stands the kids teetered on top of to and from the car. I announced with surety that I needed to be in a less taxing position to allow me to concentrate on getting pregnant. Wait, that didn't come out as I intended. What I meant was – I thought that it was a silly idea to continue in a job that required physical exertion should I be lucky enough to fall pregnant.

Leaving there, I started work as a temporary recep-tionist, then I scored a longer-term temporary role for a well-known Western Australian mining company. On reflection, my ADHD was glaringly obvious there, just not to me. There was no urgency to the role, nor was there much of a need either. I sat in the front office, ready to welcome a Mining Bigwig™ should they deign to show up. I wasn't required to do anything other than be there. Sounds fun, right? Not for me. I was blissfully unaware of my ADHD status and didn't know that was the reason that "doing nothing" was like torture for me. Like a good girl, I internalised the weird feelings I was having and gave an Academy Award-worthy performance of being a normal person.

The only real requirement of my time was answering the phone. At which point any semblance of a working memory I had would skip out the door, gleefully leaving me to cope on my own. For starters, I would never have a piece of paper to hand to write down names or messages. And it seemed like the pen that was in my hand mere seconds ago had dissipated into thin air. I would attempt to remember the person's name that was on the line, as well as where they were from, and whom they were calling to speak to. I'd assure them that their call was going through immediately and quickly place them on hold, wracking my brain. *They had said their name was John. Or was it James? From Peter's Plumbing. Or Paul's Plants. Shit.*

Sheepishly, I would return to the caller and pretend I was asking for confirmation of their name, not that I hadn't even listened in the first place. I'd then place them back on hold, promptly forget again and repeat the same process. Eventually, after a ridiculous amount of to-and-froing, we'd reach the point where it was getting awkward so I would transfer the call. Usually, the calls were for the CEO, and now I shall bequeath to you the finesse with which I delivered these calls:

"Hi Alessandro*, I have um... umm... John... from... no, sorry, it was Paul... no, it WAS John, from... um... could you ask him?"

*Name changed to protect his identity. Thought I would pick something exotic to spice things up.

Imagine being a MASSIVE CEO™ and having the temporary receptionist put several thousand calls through like that. To his credit, he was entirely affable about it. I suppose he knew I was temporary, so he probably wasn't too invested in how badly I passed the calls on. I knew I was terrible at it, but I didn't beat myself up about it. I just thought it was mildly amusing and didn't give it more than a passing thought.

About 4 weeks later I found out I was pregnant, and projectile vomiting commenced from morning to night. When I wasn't throwing up, I felt queasy. The only thing that made me feel better was food, preferably junk food. I had to enforce strict once-a-week parameters around my McDonald's intake otherwise that would have been my sole source of nutrition. I had no choice but to wrap up the temporary work and stay at home. This was the first of many times in my life where I would assume that staying at home was the answer to my problems. It was, without a doubt, an incorrect assumption.

> **" *It's not the busy that's making me struggle. It's the ADHD.* "**

Somewhere along my merry way through life I had received a message that when you're struggling, you apply an immediate cease and desist letter to yourself. That the only conceivable solution is solitude and a self-imposed timeout. I have since learnt that does *not* always work for me. It's not the busy that's making me struggle. It's the ADHD.

But ADHD wasn't an acronym in my vocabulary. Being at home wore thin with an alarming briskness, and as soon as I graduated from constant vomiting to a garden-variety all-day nausea instead, I went back to temporary work. As my pregnancy progressed, it delighted me to see people's eyes pop out when their interim receptionist rocked up with a basketball strapped to her front. But I was confident and filled spots easily. It was fun going to different jobs. Hello, undiagnosed ADHD. I was catering to my needs without realising it.

In May 2009, along came my first beautiful, big son. He was 11 days overdue, something which is still indicative of his personality now. He takes his time and likes spending time with his mama. Given my experience with childcare and nannying, I had spent his pregnancy feeling arrogantly smug about just how easy this mum gig was going to be for me.

My foray into motherhood shocked the shit out of me. Suddenly, I was a mama to a baby, and I had nothing to occupy my mind apart from that gorgeous little boy. All the arrogance was knocked clean out of my head because this baby was determined to stick to his own secret schedule, one that I was not privy to. Undeterred, I set about making it my mission to get him to do exactly what I wanted him to do. *Insert maniacal laughter here.*

Oh, how the seasoned parents laugh at my naivety.

I was in a town far away from my support system, and I was frightened. My heart was now precariously living outside of my body in the form of a baby who did *not* do what I wanted. There was not one part of my previous life left; washed away in an avalanche of baby vomit. Five years later when his brother was born, I realised that what I thought was "out of control" was a little baby who slept through the night from a week old. If I'd had my ADHD boy first, it would have been so much more of a blindside. To the mamas who had their ADHD kids as their first, I take my hat off to you. And my bra too because that shit is uncomfortable.

I kept a diary of all his statistics for each day. I obsessively documented his feeds, including what time he started and finished feeding, his sleeps, his wees and his poos. I'm talking time, size... whatever detail I could garner. I repeated this behaviour when I had my second son. I've ascertained now that it was my way of trying to maintain a modicum of control over the situation. My brain was so under-stimulated that I needed to do *something*. It gave me solace to track these daily occurrences. It gave me a somewhat tenuous sense of purpose. If I could get this kid through the day, and there was documentation saying I had done it, then the only conceivable conclusion was that maybe I was doing something right.

So, I was a stay-at-home mum. A week or so after his birth, I felt confident enough to leave the house. It wasn't until we were in the local shopping centre that a feeling of dread washed over me. The crowds became menacing, like they were looming towards us, threatening my tiny son. I couldn't believe I had been so foolish, to think I was capable of being out in public with my small baby. He was defenceless, and some idiot had made the mistake of leaving him in my incompetent care.

I looked beseechingly at other mothers, but they all moved with an air of superiority that was well out of my grasp. I tried to convince myself that one day I would look back on this and laugh, but the journey from where I was to where they were stretched in front of me like a horizon-less pilgrimage. My breaths were becoming increasingly shallow, and I knew with sudden clarity that I was going to die. Right there, in front of the butcher's shop.

There he was. My adversary, Panic Attack.

I had at least one panic attack as a child. One stands out anyway. Around 8 years old, I'd just watched *The Witches*, a movie featuring scary witches who are identifiable by their purple eyes. I'd been playing a hockey game and managed to convince myself that the umpire had purple eyes and was therefore, irrefutably, a witch. People assumed I was having an asthma attack, but it was indeed a dipping of my toes into the world of anxiety.

Nineteen years later, there I was in the middle of the shops, clutching at my chest, unable to draw a breath. I stumbled blindly to the health food shop and bought a bottle of Rescue Remedy, forcing myself to dispense the recommended droplets when I would have preferred to chug the lot. I beat a hasty path through the crowds to the safety of my car. The panic attack had defeated me.

I couldn't reconcile my idea of what motherhood should be like with this unforeseen turn of events. I was so used to being in control of my life, but now I had to consider someone else. I didn't know it, but I had survived to this point according to a strict set of rules, ones that kept me feeling safe and secure. It was a devastating oversight that they had discharged us from the hospital without giving my baby or me the rulebook.

I looked back longingly on memories of working in childcare. It was easy then. I was blithely unaware of what the children's parents faced away from the centre. All I knew was that the children in my care slept when I said and ate when I said. And if they didn't then I handed them over to the next carer. That luxury was a distant recollection. At the end of each day, my partner would come home, but during the day it was just me, and I wasn't coping. It appeared that we'd made a mutual agreement that I was the one who would be solely responsible for the night times too – I must have missed that conversation.

I was angry a lot of the time. I often felt this sensation of being out of control. And in the juxtaposition that is motherhood, I also felt indescribable joy. He was my little mate, and I loved him with a primal fierceness. I just couldn't fathom how to live with both the joy and the terror at the same time.

We made it to his first birthday intact. It was a year since I had worked, and I was desperately trying to fill my time. I would put him in his pram and walk the 90-minute round trip to the gym so I could put him in the crèche for an hour while I exercised. I did not have to walk – I had a car. It was an attempt to jam my days full of activities because the thought of sitting in the four walls of my house without anything to stimulate me was unbearable. What wasn't apparent to me at the time was that this kind of thing was a tool I had designed to cope. The issue was that it wasn't enough; I was still not managing.

I concluded that I needed a break from being a mummy for one day a week, and that I would put my little man into a childcare centre. I knew the benefits, for children and their parents, of childcare, but I still found this decision achingly difficult. I didn't want to be a "failure" (eye roll), and I was worried about what other people would think (eyes have rolled completely into the back of my head).

Despite that, I still booked him in. One glorious day a week. The first time I drove away from the centre I bawled my eyes out. *There was no WAY these people would be able to look after him! What was I THINKING!?* I was all set to drive back and get him, but then I got a grip on myself, grabbed a coffee and took a breath.

Did putting him in childcare help me feel more in control? Big fat no. Was I calm and rested after my day alone? Also no. Keep an eye out for my next book: *Things I Thought Would Fix Me But Didn't*.

Nevertheless, while it didn't initially serve the intended purpose, it *was* the catalyst for me finding the thing that got me through the next 8 years. Sewing.

Talks too much!

A love affair begins

TRIGGER WARNING – Pregnancy loss.

Now that my little man was regularly attending childcare, I had all the time to sit back and relax and enjoy some quiet time. However, as I was starting to realise, the idea of sitting around doing nothing did not equate to me feeling settled and relaxed. On the contrary, it left me feeling untethered and uncomfortable. I had always been creative, so I filled my time by learning how to crochet and then selling what I made on Facebook. I started off selling to friends and family, and then expanded my client base to complete strangers.

We had been trying to conceive a sibling for my son, but I didn't even realise I was pregnant again until the bleeding started mid-cycle. I sat on the couch with heartburn and thought, *Hmm, that's weird! The last time I had heartburn I was pregnant.*

A pregnancy test confirmed my suspicions, but the bright-red blood betrayed any excitement I may have felt. I rushed to the hospital and was informed it was ectopic; I would need surgery, and I would lose one of my fallopian tubes. It felt a little easier to process because I had no attachment to the pregnancy, but still, I was left feeling empty and melancholy. I had no way of knowing that this was the beginning of 3 years of secondary unexplained infertility. Interesting fact: you can still get pregnant with one fallopian tube – the remaining one does double duty. Clever, huh?

My mum flew over from Adelaide to be with me while I recuperated. On a trip to the local craft store, she bought me a sewing machine, as a distraction I suppose, but our family has a long history of sewing so it felt like a natural step from crocheting. I felt a glimmer of something other than the bleakness I had been shrouded in. It didn't take long for me to realise that I could sew things in the fraction of time it took to crochet, and I threw myself with merciless abandon into learning how to sew.

Hello, hyperfocus. Welcome. Not that I knew it had a name. At the time, I just knew I had found something that would alleviate the chaos inside my head and body. I taught myself everything about sewing from YouTube videos, just like I had when I learnt to crochet. And as with memorising crochet stitches, I couldn't quite understand why I had to repeatedly play the same sections 437 times before the information would finally sink in.

Nevertheless, I wasn't deterred and quickly became proficient. The irony of me teaching myself was that my mum, while not only an amazing person, is also a qualified seamstress. Yes, she could have taught me. No, I insisted on doing it all by myself.

My Facebook business page grew, particularly when I hosted two large charity auctions on my page. It was so much easier to build your followers quickly and organically back then, and I was quickly over 3,000... 5,000... 10,000 followers. I was a boy mum, but I had a knack for creating delightfully frilly baby clothing. People seemed to flock to my page because what I was making was different and gorgeous. I found it easy to put unusual fabric selections together that technically should not work, but I had this sixth sense for what would be a big seller. I sold everything I made in minutes.

Handmade was no longer the weird, knitted jumpers of old. Handmade was the place to be, and in Australia, I was one of the best. At one stage I was the biggest seller on Etsy in my category in Australia. I had a thriving business, and I was firmly ensconced in my element.

I worked.

Holy shit, did I work. By this time my big boy was in childcare 2, then 3 days a week. He attended with his two best mates, whom he is still best buds with now. On those days I would take him to childcare at 7am, work the whole day, pick him up – do the mum thing – then as soon as he was in bed I started working again until 2 or 3am.

He woke at 4:45am. Every. Single. Day. I was surviving on a few hours of sleep a night, but I did not feel it. I was so deeply in love with what I was doing that it didn't matter. I was passionate, engaged and, quite frankly, bordering on obsessed. It was all I thought about and all I talked about. I remember this feeling of pure joy whenever I was sewing or whenever I could corral someone to talk their ear off about it. I was vaguely aware that I was talking about it excessively, but I was an unstoppable force.

Fortunately, I am smart and have chosen to surround myself with exemplary friends. And I was lucky enough to be born into an incredibly supportive family. My family listened indulgently to my monologues and my friends became my customers.

Sewing was more than just the act itself. Hunched feverishly in front of my sewing machine was the place I felt most myself. I knew where every stitch would fall, safe in the knowledge that when my bare foot pressed the pedal, magic would be the indisputable result. Mistakes could be happily unpicked and reconstructed. In a world that I had been finding so uncertain, I had stumbled across a tangible commodity that was proof I was good at something. It felt like a faithful friend, later seeing me through four rounds of IVF and horrible online bullying. Eventually, it helped me ignore my relationship falling apart. Sewing was absolutely my best and most reliable friend; the one thing I knew would be there for me no matter what.

I built a fiercely loyal customer base that I cherished and who loved me back. Those women knew how to spend, and they selflessly supported a small business owner who was sewing for her life.

I worked and I worked, and I worked.

My creative side had an insatiable appetite, and I was all too happy to feed it delicious fabrics and haberdashery. I excelled at customer service, and I could manage my own website. But there were areas that I struggled with. I would have to peel myself reluctantly away from the source of my inspiration to pack orders. Strangely, people wanted their purchases sent to them. How terribly outlandish of them!

Packing and posting the orders was so draining for me. I know now that the hyperfocus was the sewing and creating, and the minutiae of packing and posting the orders was enough to tip me firmly into the land of I Can't Be Bothered. It required far too much concentration on something that wasn't rewarding me with a buzz. Sometimes I would pay my friend Leonie to come and pack the orders. That weirdo enjoyed it.

Hyperfocus

Can you relate? I did not know the word or concept of hyperfocus at the time. I did not know about dopamine. I did not know that this was my way of coping. If you'd asked me at the time, I wouldn't have been able to articulate what the issue was. I knew I was struggling, but I thought that was how motherhood was supposed to feel. I was oblivious to the way my relationship was declining. There was no life-o-meter to measure up to, so I ploughed on.

Hyperfocus is an incredibly fascinating symptom of ADHD. Obviously, with a condition that contains the words attention and deficit, you could be forgiven for thinking that people with ADHD can't concentrate. And, in part, you're right. We do struggle to concentrate on things that are of no interest to us. Our brains don't do things in the same way that neurotypical people's do. It is not that neurotypical people are "normal" or better. For people with a neurotypical nervous system, being interested in the task, or challenged, or finding the task novel or engaging is helpful, but it is not a prerequisite for doing it.

Neurotypical people use three different factors to decide what to do, how to get started on it, and to stick with it until it is completed:

1. They think they should get it done (the concept of importance).

2. They are motivated by the fact that their parents, teacher, boss, or someone they respect thinks the task is important to tackle and to complete (the concept of secondary importance).

3. They know they will get something good for doing it, or something bad will happen if they don't (the concept of rewards for doing a task and consequences/punishments for not doing it).

People with ADHD can't use the idea of importance or rewards to start and do a task. We know what's important, we like rewards, and we don't like punishment. But for us, the things that motivate the rest of the world are just annoying hassles. This explains why attempting to use reward charts or punishing ADHD children rarely works. Those things are neurotypical responses to someone who is not capable of benefiting or learning from them. It explains why so many ADHD children have an issue with the standard schooling system, or adults with ADHD struggle to work in a typical 9–5 job. Both situations are based around doing things that a person of seniority thinks is important or relevant, not what we as people think is important.

Even though many researchers believe that ADHD stems from a defective or deficit-based nervous system, I believe there is nothing wrong with our nervous system. Our nervous system works just fine when we can play by our own set of rules. When I am engaged in something I enjoy and want to do, no one can compete with my concentration, dedication or effort. It's not that I can't do other things – I am fully capable – it's just that my brain just damn well does not want to do it. So, I may appear disorganised or lazy to an employer, but it's just that my brain can't place the level of importance onto a task that matters to them.

> **❝ I was essentially using my hyperfocus to create my own dopamine. ❞**

When someone with ADHD finds something they are truly interested in, they can achieve a level of highly focused attention that lasts a long time. I know that I can concentrate on something so hard that I lose track of everything else going on around me. Hyperfocus sounds awesome, right? And it is – but it's also selective. My brain doesn't go, *Let's hyperfocus on this work we need to get done today.* Nope. My brain goes, *Let's write 2,000 words of your book in an hour while ignoring the work you should be doing because, you know, it's your job.*

I wrote about 60 percent of this book while I was supposed to be working. In my defence, the job was exhaustingly snore-worthy. Until that point I had lived my life at breakneck speed, finishing tasks in record time. So, the change from that to calm was unnerving. Writing this book was the stimulation I needed, ironically, to do well at my job. By feeding my brain something stimulating, it gave me the ability to then focus on tasks that were not rewarding to me. But that my boss insisted I do. Rude.

The hyperfocus of my sewing helped me through arduous times. I was unconsciously using hyperfocus as a coping mechanism for what I now know were ADHD symptoms. I knew something was up, I just didn't know what. I wasn't aware that my brain had abnormally low levels of dopamine – a neurotransmitter – and norepinephrine – a hormone and neurotransmitter. They are responsible for helping us to feel pleasure, satisfaction and motivation. I had no way of knowing that I was essentially using my hyperfocus to create my own dopamine.

Is it any wonder I didn't want to stop, or that it was all I wanted to talk about? I was fortunate enough to make money from my hyperfocus. Being in a state of hyperfocus feels so good to me. I am so glad that I get to have a brain that allows me to do that. When I can harness it, I can achieve some cool shit.

The only thing about hyperfocus is that you can't rely on it. It's not something you can access whenever you want to. And often it concludes without warning, so that thing you were in the middle of doing is left unfinished. It would be easy to be hard on yourself for this and think about how much time and money you've wasted on various hyperfocuses. I don't think like that because I've already moved on to the next hyperfocus, so that's for yesterday me to worry about.

Writing this book snuck up on me as a hyperfocus. I started casually documenting my experiences, right from my suspicions about ADHD. At first it was only ever supposed to be a blog. It didn't take long for me to realise that I had a lot to say!

This is how my son ended up with a full gaming computer setup in his room. The very gaming setup that I sat at and wrote the other 40 percent of this book. I didn't have anywhere to write properly before then, unless I was at work writing while I was supposed to be working. At home I was sitting scrunched up on the couch with the laptop balanced precariously on my lap. I decided that my son needed a brand-new gaming desk, keyboard and a suspiciously comfortable gaming chair that just happened to have a wonderful back support, perfect for Mum! What a coincidence!

I was unprepared for the way the words in this book have *poured* out of me. Writing is a means of catharsis. It's given me a chance to pull the swirling thoughts from my brain and place them on a page. I can feel myself producing dopamine because it's when I am writing that I feel something else on top of my medication. It's elusive, but when it appears I roll with it.

Learning about hyperfocus was one of my "holy shit, it has a name" realisations that came with my ADHD diagnosis. It also explained why, as I went through life un-diagnosed, I was not able to gain anywhere near the same sense of pleasure as I did when I was creative. There was just one problem, and it was a big one. I encountered this problem after years of fixating on my sewing.

Burnout.

But it took me a few years to get there. And a lot happened along the way.

Talks too much!

Being myself

By this time in my life, I'd had my second son, the little firecracker. Remember how I said I used to work until 2 or 3am and then get up and do it again? That doesn't work when you have two kids, one of whom doesn't consistently go to sleep at the same time or sleep through the night. Or nap in the day. My eldest would snooze for at least 2 hours every day. He napped until he was 5, to the point that I was worried about how he was going to make it through the day at school without a sleep. My younger ADHD son gave up naps at 18 months old. And the naps he had taken before that were hit and miss; you never knew what you were going to get on any given day.

I had worked so hard to build my business up and had enjoyed considerable success. I didn't want to start my youngest in childcare too young, so naps became my bread and butter. When they didn't exist, I simply couldn't work. There was a limit to how late I could stay up too as the lack of sleep was catching up with me. My bones were aching with fatigue.

But money was tight – I needed to be bringing in an income. On I soldiered, the hyperfocus becoming slightly frayed at the edges. Dissolution was sniffing around the edges too, its presence ushered in by the necessity to earn a living that was now attached. Not to mention my relationship was steadily headed towards its unavoidable death. It was as if the fog of young children settled a little, we looked at each other and thought, *I don't even know who you are.* Distance stretched between us.

> 66 *I was trapped on a vicious merry-go-round, and I wanted off.* 99

I developed a lovely jaw-clenching habit. I had a permanent twitch in my eye, which would alternate with the blooming of a sty. I acquired a mysterious bout of what seemed like vertigo, but an extreme version, where the world would tip on its axis unpredictably with a *whoosh* and next minute I would be on my hands and knees desperately trying to get myself to the toilet before I vomited. It would take hours for the spinning to stop. Interestingly, it was worse when I was stressed. I was trapped on a vicious merry-go-round, and I wanted off.

Gazing into the mirror, I would look at the unrecognisable girl reflected there, and all I could think was, *I'm miserable.*

After a 10-year relationship, the boys' dad and I reached breaking point. It was amicable – the days of anger and recrimination were behind us – and we had been rattling around in the empty shell of affiliation for a year. I took the boys, aged 1½ and 6½ and moved out. That's the simplified version of an incredibly difficult time.

Now I was on my own, and I had to make this work even more than before. My little one started in childcare, and I had some autonomy back. I found my sew-jo again and hit the ground running with my business. The hyper-focus was back and my business expanded with swift and wild abandon. I had seven women working for me in various roles, and I was kicking business goals.

I threw myself into online dating and spent the next while just having a ripsnorter of a time. I am entirely sure this is a universal fact: so many weird people are on dating apps. It was like being on a gameshow, only usually people on gameshows don't pretend they've lost their wallet and then disappear after you've paid. By no means do I expect the man to pay but going halves would have been nice. Nevertheless, I doggedly persevered, clinging to the hope that because I was on there, maybe another normal person would be too.

I had gone on a first date with a guy who, quite frankly, did nothing for me. It was a sign of how far my standards had dropped that I was at home, getting ready to go on a second date with him. While I was doing my face, I had this niggling feeling that I shouldn't go. I had arranged a babysitter though, so I pushed the feeling aside. Well, my instincts were offended, so much so that my body flooded with a feeling of dread. I broke out in a sweat and felt queasy. True story. It's entirely possible that I would have pushed through anyway – a night out is a night out – but Kismet stepped in, and the guy cancelled the date.

There I was, rattling around my house, the babysitter already on the couch with the kids. *Stuff it, I'm going out.* A right swipe on Tinder led me to connect with a dashing gentleman called Neil. We messaged briefly, matching each other with above-average banter. When he suggested we should meet for a drink some time, I replied, "We should – like now?"

Arriving at our first date, despite my bravado, I wasn't in a peachy-keen headspace. To be more accurate, my confidence was in tatters. So, when I saw him waiting for me at the bar and he was SO handsome, I thought there was no way he would like me. My self-worth-o-meter was so low that I would have struggled to fish it out of a well.

There's no chance he'll be attracted to me... I may as well be myself then! I thought.

I'm not sure what the other option was. A pretend version of myself, I guess. One that fits the mould of the perfect girl. I had been given negative feedback from partners over the years: I was too much, or too loud; that I had too much to say. I had spent my adult life trying to be someone I wasn't, and look how that turned out. I had slowly become a shell of myself. Clearly, that wasn't the answer.

I figured I had nothing to lose with this guy as I'd already written myself off for him. What a gross disservice I was doing myself. And if this resonates with you, then I am sorry. I am sorry to myself for thinking this about me. The thing is it allowed me to let down all my defences, and I was 100 percent me. Throughout the date, we laughed so much that my face ached. Turns out, I am fucking awesome when I'm me.

Somehow, against all odds, I had landed the jackpot. From the get-go, this man soothed my soul. Our relationship blossomed and it was a grand old time. My boys would go to their dad's place every second weekend, and I would head to Neil's for a weekend of child-free bliss. Neil is a patient, kind and gentle man who absolutely takes the piss out of me. Seems like an oxymoron, I know, but there is never any malice – we both enjoy the schtick. Most of all, he *likes* me. The actual me. Not a fake version I made up to keep someone happy. I don't have to pretend with him. He makes me feel safe and appreciated, and we laugh about everything. He is my teammate, my best friend, and I hope no one is offended by this but he's the only person I never get sick of.

My sewing business continued, but by now something had changed – the magic was ebbing away. I didn't have the same fire and I felt burnt out. I longed for the sanctuary of a steady pay cheque. With these feelings not going away, I decided it was time, after 8 years, to head back to the workforce.

Talks too much!

The time the shit hiteth the fan

TRIGGER WARNING – Panic attacks.

It had been a decade since I had been in the "real" workforce, so for my re-entry I took what I perceived to be an easy role in the building trade. It was a part-time role in reception and data entry. It was simple, but you needed to be accurate, which I was. Mistakes would cost the company tens of thousands of dollars. I found the work monotonous, but I was still sewing on my days off, keeping my creative urges sated. It gave me a sense of security knowing when and how much I would be getting paid each week. The downside was that one of the bosses was a misogynistic prick. I was on his good side because I did not make mistakes. Until I did.

The other receptionist left, and I somehow ended up doing her job *and* mine. The weight sat upon my shoulders. The pressure wasn't an issue – I could always rise to the occasion and prided myself on being close to perfect, regardless of the personal cost. Gradually, that cost crept higher, and the load became uncomfortable around my neck.

I had such high expectations of myself – higher than any employer could ever have – and those expectations were so lofty that I preferred pushing through anything to ensure I maintained a ridiculously elevated level of expectation on myself. If I made a mistake, I took it so badly that I would beat myself up over it, for days. Being chastised by a superior was a doddle. I was a much harsher critic than anyone else could ever be.

Now, let us just remember that I was, at this point, undiagnosed with ADHD, carrying out two roles, in a high-pressure industry, with my own elevated expectations and a narcissistic boss. Sounds relaxing, doesn't it? Now I know that burnout occurs for adults with ADHD when they take on too many things to try to prove themselves. At the time I saw it as a personal flaw. The situation deteriorated and mistakes started slipping through my tight grasp. I was on a wobbly, loose tightrope with no safety net. And when I fell, it was catastrophic.

On the flipside, my personal life could not have been better. After a year of courtship, Neil helped me and the boys move into a new house. It felt so natural having him there that I asked him to move in too. The transition was smooth, and we settled into a new life together. For the first time, I was ensconced in a relationship with someone who (capital L) LOVED me. So, there I was, feeling adored and being adoring. My boys had welcomed him into the fold, and I was sinking into the feeling of being safe and secure.

Without warning, one night something triggered inside of me, and I had the biggest panic attack I had ever had in my life. But my body wasn't done with one. I had hundreds of them, all throughout the night. They continued for weeks; multiple panic attacks, day and night. I couldn't sleep. Food tasted like cardboard. It was as though I was running on a motor of fear. I feared the panic attacks, and the fear then ironically caused more. I was in a constant state of agitation, and I felt like there was never going to be an end. It lasted for weeks. I was a walking, talking mess who was parading as if nothing was wrong.

> ❝ *Everything that had hurt me and caused me pain could no longer be contained.* ❞

I tried to explain to Neil and my family what was going on, but I didn't really let them see the horror that was wracking my body every moment. Somehow, I still dragged myself to work and pretended. I looked after my children under a façade. My inner self was in tatters. I was on a ghost train and the exit signs had been painted over.

I look back now and I truly believe that because I felt so safe in my relationship, I could allow everything I had been carrying around with me to finally come to the surface. All those things I had been stuffing back down. Everything that had hurt me and caused me pain could no longer be contained. It all came out, and I was on my knees.

Daily I would make myself take a walk around the block. I would try to be mindful. I would listen to podcasts and meditations, and I would try to relax. My body was trying to tell me something but the shock of finally being at the mercy of myself was too much for the lesson to be learnt then. All the control I had maintained over my life was gone. I had two children that I couldn't let down. I was working in a soul-sucking job, and I was dying.

I found an amazing psychologist who taught me about how my brain worked and why it was reacting in the way it was. We revisited childhood stuff and relationship stuff. One of the best things she said to me was, "You're not going to be coming to see me for long. I'm going to give you the tools you need to get back out there and live your life."

And she was right. Through a combination of talking therapy and eye movement desensitisation and reprocessing (EMDR) therapy, we extricated and examined the reactions I was having. It allowed me to breathe again. Gradually, things eased, and I was able to use tools to help me get through.

I went from having full-blown, unmanageable, crippling anxiety to still having run-of-the-mill anxiety. I was prepared to accept this watered-down version because it was preferable to what I had just been through. What I was hiding, though, was that I was still always on the precipice of the cliff of succumbing to a panic attack. I had to constantly monitor myself to stay on top of this lurking feeling that I was one moment away from going back to the bleak place. On the outside it looked like I had pulled through. But I was hiding a dark secret.

The fantastic thing about getting therapy was that it allowed me to see that the job I had been doing was not good for me. While I found it difficult to admit that it had beaten me, I told Neil that I wanted to quit. He was supportive, and I handed in my notice the next day. I went back to sewing, but the magic wasn't just gone, it was dead and buried. I realise now that the hyperfocus had burnt itself out. I was burnt out. However, my bills didn't care about burnout; they still had to get paid. Guuuurl, time for another job!

Burnout, again!

I landed a job that seemed to fit with my abilities and school hours well and with an innovative company. The job was incredibly fast-paced, and I was under high pressure. Typically, when I start in a new role, I am unstoppable. My desire to prove myself, combined with my competitive streak, gives me an edge. Employers are wowed by me as I zip effortlessly through the assigned tasks. Never mind that this time I was a rotten mess on the inside! I was receiving positive feedback while ignoring the complete lack of balance in any other area of my life, so that's okay!

I can look back now and realise that while my ADHD made things difficult, I was still achieving exceptional results. I increased sales from $500 per month to over $4,000 per month. I gave their social media an overhaul. I fostered rewarding relationships with customers and added so much value to the business. I recall how I would get to work and literally feel that "head down, bum up" mentality go over me, and I would smash through the work. I was the go-to person, I was the jack of all trades, and if there was an issue it would come to me.

For a while it was satisfying to get to the end of the day and look back at all the fires I had put out, to look at the business growing and know I was an integral part of that. Hunkered down in the back corner of my mind was the truth, purposefully ignored by me. The tightrope was back, wobblier than ever, only this time I had to sing and juggle at the same time.

I began to see that my "perfectionism" was coming back to bite me on the arse. I said yes to everything because I didn't know how to say that I didn't have the capacity to take on extra things. I was completely time blind, and my overzealous optimism meant that I genuinely believed I could fit everything in. I would have chosen to walk across hot coals rather than have anyone think I was less than capable.

During this time, I was doing lots of self-reflection, and I started to implement some changes. I didn't realise then that these things were ADHD related, but I came to see that I had an issue with setting boundaries and being realistic about what I could manage to do in the time I had to do it. I had been painfully singed with the double responsibility at the last job and I wasn't about to do it again.

I still had no idea about my diagnosis. I just thought that I needed to try harder. Despite my desire to set limits in my new workplace, carrying that out was another story. The feeling of tension that I had been carrying for some time now was building. I was in a constant state of fight or flight, and I could not take a step back and evaluate. I felt on edge, ready to lose my shit at any given moment.

My chest was tight, my jaw was constantly aching, and my stomach was in knots. Leaving work for the day, it wouldn't have mattered if someone tried to mug me – my body was so rigid they'd have bounced off me.

At home I would sit on the couch and feel an unbridled energy running rampant through my muscles. From the outside I was sitting watching TV, but, on the inside, I was a manic mess – competing thoughts piling over each other in their desire to be heard. My jaw was tight from clenching, and I felt like I needed to move. But that was such a weird thing to do, so instead I would just sit there, locked in my own personal hell. I was still affected by my breakdown and was in constant fear that it would rear its ugly head again. I assumed that this was what anxiety felt like.

At work, I approached my manager to talk about the lack of help and support I was receiving. She suggested that I just needed to have better time management, that I needed to be more organised, or I needed to make sure I used the Outlook calendar. None of this was ground-breaking. How many times had I bought a pretty planner, sure that *this* was the one that was going to make me organised? Until I lost it. Or spilt water on it. Or simply never filled it out.

I LOVE a planner. Love them. Do not use them, but I bloody love them. The ones that come with cute little stickers and matching smelly pastel pens?! Ugh – K I L L M E. I will buy you and I WILL never use you. But the whispered promise at the back of my mind that this would be the one that worked was too much to ignore and impulse control would beat a hasty retreat, leaving me unsupervised and spending unnecessary cash.

The idea of the Outlook calendar appealed to me immensely. I happily put appointments and reminders on there. The fatal flaw was that I just did not ever register the reminder when it came up on the screen. It didn't matter if I was sitting at the screen and working on something. The reminder would pop up, directly into my blind spot – I quite literally could not see it.

I found so many helpful apps, but how would I ever remember to look at them? Instead, I would use reminders and alarms on my phone. I didn't give too much thought as to why I needed to do these things. I just accepted that this was how I was, and this was the only way I could stay on top of my life.

I could feel burnout licking at the edges. Again. The divide between work and my personal life was murky. I had become so indispensable that they couldn't operate without me. I would get phone calls after hours and on my days off. Sick days were met with a stony reaction. My manager was becoming increasingly hostile, and I couldn't see a way out, so I started looking for another role. I wanted to do the right thing, so I let them know, at which point my manager did a backflip and begged me to stay.

> **" Can you see that red ADHD flag
> flapping merrily in the breeze? "**

I doubled down on my desire to start setting bound-aries, so I agreed to stay on the proviso that I would only work 3 days a week. And they would pay me more. To my surprise, they agreed. I would come to see that my attempt to claw back some balance was a double-edged sword – on one side was the relief of working fewer days, but on the other side were my employers, who did not replace me on the other two days for months. And when they did it was with someone who created more work for me with their incompetence.

I was back in the same situation I had been in my last role. Trying to do the work of a full-time person in part-time hours. Of course, I know it's the employer's responsibility to replace me, and I shouldn't be the one compensating for that. Try telling that to an overachieving, highly-strung people-pleaser who was operating solely on anxiety. I somehow found reserves within myself that meant it looked like the role was still operating as before. With 40 percent less time. Cool cool cool cool cool cool cool cool cool. Why would they bother replacing me? I was running myself into the ground, thereby eliminating the need for someone else.

This wasn't apparent immediately. All I knew was that I had 2 days a week to myself. Time to unwind and luxuriate in my abundance of free time, right? No. I had too much free time now and that was intolerable. Instead of taking up my rightful place as a Lady of Leisure, I did what anyone would do and signed up to study a Certificate IV in Community Services. Anyone? Anyone? Bueller?

And here's the kicker. I didn't sign up because I had much interest in using the certification to work in community services. I signed up because *I wanted something to do*. Other people take up a hobby. I start a 12-month course. Can you see that red ADHD flag flapping merrily in the breeze? At the time it seemed perfectly reasonable. Now I can look back on that and see I was desperately trying to fill my aching brain with something that would stimulate enough dopamine for me to feel fulfilled. The satisfaction I had initially experienced at my current job was slowly being overshadowed by a ridiculous workload, an unsupportive boss and this unrelenting feeling that I needed to get out.

I could only concur that this constant tension I felt was a result of my job. There was only one thing for it. I needed a boring job, one where I could just slow right down and just chill. Right?

Talks too much!

With boredom comes diagnosis

I have this funny way of saying things and then they come true. Call it manifestation, call it luck, call it whatever you want... just call me. *Boom-tish.* Sure enough, I did land that undemanding job. It was a cushy full-time role at a university in clinical research. Because it is a superb idea to transition to full-time when you are studying and already feeling swamped. There they are again – the ADHD traits of time blindness and overcommitting.

I started work and the job was exactly what I'd asked for. Snooze Town. Wonderful. Now I could get on with the bizness of relaxing in my undemanding job.

You can imagine my complete and utter shock when it became painful to be faced with such banality. My body was so uncomfortable with my brain being under-stimulated that I couldn't stop moving. I felt like I had to stretch, move and wriggle my body because I felt prickly with the *nothing*. At one point I was stretching at my desk and I slowly slid onto the ground from my chair. A 39-year-old woman slithering to the floor. In a professional role. Where someone could walk in the door.

And it's not that I didn't have work to do. I did. It's just that no matter what I did, I could *not* get my brain to do it. I knew I was intellectually able to do the work. They were being nice to me and allowing me to ease my way in. So it wasn't that I had too much to do either. It's just that what they gave me to do was the last thing on earth I wanted to do. I ached with unwelcome internal mutiny.

My brain had never rebelled against me like this before. You couldn't have paid me to do my work. Okay, so they WERE paying me to do it but that wasn't enough. It turns out that the field I was in wasn't interesting to me. I thought that because it was a "good job", I would then just show up and be a "good worker".

One of the requirements of my role was to attend meetings and take minutes. Meetings where it appeared that everyone was speaking another language. I quickly learned to record the meetings on voice notes on my phone. Cool hack, huh? Yeah, it works. Unless you're like me and listening back to it and attempting to type up what people are saying takes around 10 times longer than the actual meeting does because your working memory is so poor. Or, if you're also like me and lose interest quickly in the meeting. You've blended into the background anyway, so you proceed to start playing on the same phone that is recording the meeting. And then when you listen back to it all you can hear is the sound of you fiddling with the phone, drowning out the meeting. Professional, that's me.

The blandness was EXCRUCIATING.

This was the first time in my adult life that I'd been faced with such empty monotony. Being bored had always seemed like such a lovely concept. As a mother with two young boys who play a ridiculous amount of sport, and having worked in high-pressure jobs, I had ached for the enticing lull of the humdrum. Surely, if I got to the point of being unbusy, I would finally be able to relax? That ever-present feeling of being knackered would disappear. But here I was – finally bored – and slinking onto the floor like a 7-year-old boy...

Wait a minute...

My mind flitted over the thought I'd had one year ago when my son was diagnosed. I had been reading up on the symptoms and I'd thought:

Doesn't everyone feel like that?

I looked around the office. All the academics and administration staff were working diligently. In fact, now that I thought about it, they always did that. And they did tend to look bewildered when I interrupted them to ask a question after doing a silly walk across the office. But was I asking necessary questions? If I'm perfectly honest, no. Sometimes it was just to tell them a random thing that had happened to me, a thought that had popped into my head or because a funny bird went past the window.

My Google history:

Signs of ADHD in women

Women with ADHD

ADHD diagnosis later in life

Late diagnosis ADHD

How tall is Tom Cruise?

How do I know if I have ADHD?

Okay, so I didn't always stay on topic. He's 170cm, by the way. I'm 170cm! I feel like his shortness has been overplayed. 170cm is not even that short! But I digress. It was becoming apparent that just a little bit, on occasion, I *may* have ADHD. And this is when impostor syndrome dropped in.

Talks too much!

Impostor syndrome

Actual thoughts my brain had:

You can't have ADHD, you did so well in school.

But it's just anxiety.

You're too old, you would have known by now.

But you've been successful with work and owned your own business.

And my favourite:

Ugh, everyone is going to think you're just copying your son. (Or was that just me?)

Yes, I thought these things, with my own brain. I know now that this is a classic example of impostor syndrome.

Impostor syndrome is a fun one. It has become more widely talked about on social media in recent times, which is great. Anything that increases knowledge and awareness is a great thing. The term impostor syndrome has been around since 1978. Not only was this the year the Space Invaders game launched (weird reference), but it was also the year that clinical psychologists Dr Pauline Clance and Suzanne Imes coined the term.

It is used to describe people who are bloody good at what they do, but they cannot always see that. People with IS (not to be confused with IBS – that is another story) often cannot recognise their accomplishments. They spend their life waiting for people to find out they are a fraud, which will not happen because they are not. They are successful because they have worked hard and made the effort.

> " *I could not wrap my head around not being able to carry out simple tasks.* "

People who suffer from IS may feel as though they just lucked their way into success. They may not be able to celebrate victories, instead looking to the next thing they need to complete. You may be only able to focus on the one thing that went wrong, instead of ALL the things that went right. You may be dismissive of compliments and praise, feeling you do not deserve them. And you may constantly compare yourself to others.

Something that ADHD people do that can exacerbate IS is hide our struggles. This may be because we've been faced with a shaming rhetoric around our actions or behaviour. Or, like me, you expected so much more of yourself that you were embarrassed that such simple things could be so insurmountable. I had spent my life being an achiever, and I could not wrap my head around not being able to carry out simple tasks. So, we work harder, and longer, because things are more difficult for us to manage. We are getting the results but at a personal cost. On the outside, we are achieving and kicking goals. Our bosses and co-workers see success, but they are not aware of what it took to get to that point.

On the surface, I had always achieved well in job roles, particularly when I had my own business. But I felt so constantly out of control with other areas that I didn't trust the wins. I was always waiting for this to be the time that they discovered it had been a fluke. I was so desperate that no one know what it was like inside my head and my body that I teetered on that tightrope with the highest expectations balanced unevenly on my shoulders. All it would take was one breeze of wind, and I would topple over.

When it came to being diagnosed, I felt as though I didn't deserve that diagnosis. While for some people the diagnosis doesn't feel great, I desperately wanted it. It answered so many questions that I had about myself. But my brain was telling me that I was making these things up about myself, even though I wasn't. It's complex and it's weird and if you're feeling like this – push through! You *are* worthy and you are not making things up.

Something extraordinary started happening after I was open about my diagnosis. Other women started to approach me and talk about their suspicions about themselves. The butterfly effect rippled through my friends, then their friends and beyond. These conversations were crucial. I got the final push to get diagnosed when a well-known entertainer that I follow on social media was open about her ADHD journey. She was so relatable to me, and it was like this switch went off where, suddenly, I realised that I wanted the clarity she had.

After my diagnosis (of which I'll go into more detail in a later chapter), I was speaking to my beautiful friend Kelsey. Kelsey and I have spoken before about her suspicions about her own ADHD. She found the courage to admit something important to me. She said, "I feel like by me pursuing my own diagnosis, I'm just riding on the coattails of your diagnosis. I feel like I'm just copying you."

And there it is. That old bastard, impostor syndrome. Kelsey is an amazingly intelligent, accomplished woman. At 41 years old, she is not only one of my ride-or-dies, but she also smashed through a Bachelor of Education while single-parenting her two children. She has nothing to gain from pretending to have ADHD. But such is the pain and shame we carry around, we don't think we are worthy of pursuing a diagnosis, *even though we KNOW something is terribly wrong.*

I could truly empathise with Kelsey's admission. As I mentioned earlier, when that well-known entertainer announced her own diagnosis it did push me to get mine. But I also had the following thoughts:

People who follow her will think I'm copying her.

People are going to think I'm trying to be part of the ADHD gang.

Yes, I had those thoughts. On repeat. In several other forms, too. In my mind, these "people" would judge me and find me wanting. I can only put it down to a deep sense of not feeling good enough, and this feeling that even though she now hummed with the luminosity of the knowing, it wouldn't work for me. I could totally understand why Kelsey had said what she had said.

Kelsey's confession showed me the incredible power of communication and how brave people are to speak up. Imagine if Kelsey hadn't felt able to discuss that with me. Imagine if she had spoken to someone else about her thoughts and they had confirmed her fears; made her think she wasn't valid? That would just be a damn shame. Impostor syndrome can be really damaging and hold you back from pursuing something that is going to help you.

I confidently wrote around 20,000 words of this book before I had an official diagnosis. And then, post diagnosis, this was what my brain was trying to tell me:

Why are you writing this book? What's the point? You're not an expert!

And this is what I tell my brain right back: *That's right. I am not an ADHD expert. I am, however, stuffing my head full of as much knowledge as I can about ADHD so I can learn about myself. Then I can share that information in this book, and people who relate to it can read it.* I believe that is a term called "research". See, if I listened to my brain, I would stop right now. I would let the IS take over and stop me from achieving something that not only do I really want to, but I have been enjoying doing and finding incredibly cathartic.

Many life coaches, motivational speakers and the like will tell you that the single most important tool for success comes from finding your why. Your why can be a unique driver to push you to achieve something extraordinary. One of my "whys" is to tell my story in the hope that by sharing my experiences, I help one other woman. Just one. Of course, I would love to help more, but that one woman is just as important to me as tons of women. And who is the expert in telling *my* story? Me!

I have unique things to say. Some of them may resonate with you and some of them may not. Just like in a job role, you can be fantastic at some things and struggle with others, but that doesn't stop you from doing the job. And I am not going to let it stop me from writing this book.

I feel like that turned into a therapy session for me and I can tell you, I ain't mad about it.

Talks too much!

Just relax

At night I would dream of organisation. I dreamt like it was my job and I had to get shit done. I frowned the whole way through my night-time visions. I dreamt that I was always one step behind. In the dreams I was trying to make phone calls, but I couldn't quite get the number right. Dreams where I was late, dreams where I lost things, dreams where it depended on me to get the task done, and no matter how hard I tried, it eluded me. I would try to run in my dreams, but I wouldn't be able to get past the first step. I would dream about wanting the night to hurry up and be over so I could stop feeling so uncomfortable in my sleep.

Every morning I would wake up with a jolt, my heart thumping in my chest. You know how people wake up leisurely in the movies? Not me. I was A-W-A-K-E. My whole body would be tensed, ready for action. Fight or flight, baby. I was stuck in a perpetual cycle of body rigidity. My jaw would be sore, and I would have clenched my teeth so hard throughout the night that it felt like my teeth were rattling in my gums. The inside of my cheeks was red raw with ulcers; the skin caught between my teeth when I ground them in my restless slumber.

I didn't just start my day – I bloody well STARTED MY DAY. *It is just anxiety*, I told myself, as I lay stiff as a board, trying desperately to listen to a spoken meditation to calm me down. *Be present*, I would whisper, as I waded through the 487,000 thoughts rushing through my head. Round and round and round. I could have several simultaneous imaginary conversations running through my head, a song on repeat and still manage to be berating myself for something I'd said or done the day before.

My chest would be heavy with an unyielding weight. My stomach would be rock-solid, with nary a sit-up responsible. But anxiety is commonplace, right? I see everyone sharing memes and making jokes about their anxiety. So, it is normal, and I should be capable of just getting on with my day. I felt confident in my assumption that loads of people felt like this.

I would get up, knowing I had to get myself ready and prompt the kids to get their butts into gear too. I would trip over something I left right next to my bed. Making my way out of the bedroom, I would survey the house in despair. Stuff was everywhere, which I found overwhelming. I decided to have a family meeting about cleaning up after ourselves, and then realised with horror that *90 percent of the mess was mine*. How could that even be? I could have sworn I did nothing BUT tidy up. The irony of being a messy person who hates mess is not lost on me.

I would wade through the jumble and swiftly be pulled in multiple directions by a cacophony of competing omnishambles. Dirty lunchboxes from the day before, nothing to make lunches with, greasy hair and unwashed dishes. Forgotten tasks from days earlier would pop up yet my reward-based brain was drawn into shopping on eBay instead of prioritising the far more pertinent chores.

It felt like I blinked once and the clock had an un-welcome 7:30am on its display. Shit. We needed to leave at 8am. The kids would be undressed, watching TV. I would explode but it would turn out that they couldn't get dressed thanks to their school uniforms still being in the washing machine, no longer clean and now creating their own little ecosystem in the dank recesses. Dirty clothes from the bathroom would be dragged on, then spritzed ineffectively with body spray. One of them would remind me that I hadn't made their lunches yet.

I would rush around the house, trying to locate lost items, activating my "lost item blindness". Not only was the item lost, but looking for it made my brain become foggy and confused as if a blackout curtain was over my eyes. The elusive item could be right in front of me, and I would be unable to see it. Lurking in the back of my mind was the feeling that even beyond these lost items, I was missing some vital thing.

Far past the allotted 8am leaving time, it would take several attempts to truly be on our way, returning for forgotten laptops, lunches, drink bottles and bags. My dogs no longer reacted to me coming back to the house. I would *finally* be on my way, and maybe I would just about get to work on time when a sudden thought would strike me. *Did I turn the stove off? Did I unplug my straightener?* I would have no choice but to turn back and check. And, almost always, they were off – but I had no memory of turning them off.

Before I went into work, I would attempt some deep breathing. Mindfulness. That was what was wrong with me, I decided. I just needed to meditate more. So, I would quickly chuck on a guided meditation from YouTube with my eyes squeezed tight while sitting in the carpark. With my chest tight, the knot in my stomach, the lingering feeling I had forgotten something and my head spinning, I would struggle desperately to stay on task, dragging my mind back from the swirling thoughts going through my head.

> ❝ *My internal screensaver led me to miss vital information.* ❞

Once at work I would try to face the endless tasks that demanded my attention, but the thought of tackling them was too overwhelming. So, I tried to ignore them. Except I couldn't because their presence throbbed behind me. I knew I should be able to carry out my duties, but I couldn't find the keys to start my motor.

I floundered through my days in this fog, anxiety humming through my body relentlessly. I remember approaching my manager at a previous job and explaining that I was struggling, but then I wouldn't be able to articulate why. All the reasoning I had in my brain would trickle away, and I would be left unsure. I had to put a sign on the back of my chair warning people not to talk to me because I was so easily distracted.

But then other times I would get a task assigned to me, like designing a website, and I would slip into a different realm where nothing else existed. I would be so focused on that job and enjoy myself so much that other, more urgent tasks would become inconsequential. Until someone followed up and I had to quickly start the neglected task and cover-up that I'd forgotten about it.

People would ask me to do things, and I would agree, but once I walked away, I would realise that I had tuned out halfway through the conversation. There was no chance I was going to go back and ask them to clarify. I would hide from the task and hope they'd forget they had asked me. My internal screensaver also activated in meetings, leading me to miss vital information. Admitting I wasn't listening or didn't understand was not an option.

By the end of the day, I was stretched taut, like a rubber band ready to snap. Driving home from work was when I really felt the tension hit me. I started associating being in the car on the way home as a negative experience. I had finished work – the pressure was off – so why were my shoulders up around my ears? Why was I holding my stomach in such a tense way?

It always surprised me that I had to prepare a meal for my children each night, and so I learnt to simplify. My kids' favourite meal became chopped-up fruit, veggies and protein – we call it a Funny Face. The witching hour was fraught and all it would take was one minor thing to tip me over the edge. I would see my kids' faces go white and shut down.

But I couldn't stop. I didn't know how to. Small problems seemed so big to me, and my carefully laid plans of being more patient and more kind would come crashing down like a precariously stacked tower of cards. I *knew* the things were not a big deal. I would be apologising seconds after I exploded. I *knew* I was being unreasonable, but I felt detached and lost. I was vulnerable and frightened, and this manifested as anger.

When the kids were asleep I would look at their beautiful faces, and that was when the internal criticism stepped up to the plate. How the *fuck* was I expecting them to grow up into great little people when I was so desperately out of control? What kind of example was I giving them? I was ruining them, and, despite my best intentions, I was continuing to lose my shit multiple times a day, followed quickly by remorseful backpedalling. But do the words really hold any impact when you go and do the same thing the next day? Nightly, I would wait until Neil fell asleep, then curl up in my bed and cry until my face was swollen and aching, vowing that the next day would be the one where it would be different.

On the weekend I would just plan to relax. On alternate weekends my boys would be with their dad, so I would plan to spend time with Neil, or just lounge around and switch off. But I could do this only after tidying the house. It wasn't feasible to me to do housework (I use the term loosely) without also listening to a podcast on my wireless headphones. And I felt like I couldn't enjoy myself if I had to look at the mess.

I was struck by this bizarre inertia. I *knew* there were things I wanted to do, but sometimes there were so many things that they paralysed me. I *knew* there were things I enjoyed doing, but they dangled enticingly just out of reach. I was driven by this internal message that there were things I *should* be doing, and I frantically searched my brain for ideas of what these were.

Sometimes, I trotted off to the nail salon and got my nails done. The nail lady would slap my hand and tell me to "Relax, dahling" because I was holding my whole body so tightly that I was either twisting my hand in complete rebellion against where she wanted it to go, or I was squeezing hers so hard I left marks. My whole body was a ball of tension. Lying on a massage table for a rare massage, I would feel as though I was levitating one inch off the table, stiff as a board and unmalleable.

I sat on the couch at night, seemingly watching a movie, but I couldn't help but pick up my phone every few minutes. I didn't even know what I was looking for. Adrenaline pumped around my body and my muscles were tense. Of course, from the outside, I was none of these things.

> ❝ *I pretended I knew what I was doing, and that I was okay.* ❞

No one knew. Some people were aware that I suffered from anxiety, but I never let on to what extent. The ridiculous juxtaposition here was that I was an open person. If I thought something, generally, I would say it. I would gladly share my surface-level daily troubles and challenges. I knew my openness paved the way for other women to share their own issues too. I didn't mind telling people almost anything that happened to me. Most things could be discussed with my mum or a trusted friend, and they could be worked through and overcome.

However, despite my open appearance, there was an inflexible line. It was inconceivable to step over it. I didn't want to acknowledge the hidden things because *they never went away*. I have always been the kind of person who struggles with asking for help. Usually, I prefer the "shutdown, go internal, figure it out on your own and then share it once it's all done and dusted" method.

I barely discussed the breakdown of my first relationship until it happened. I often retreat from my best friend until I feel ready to talk. But these were all problems that already had solutions. I could comfortably talk about them afterwards, safe in the knowledge that I had figured them out or moved past them.

It wasn't that I didn't have trusted friends and family because I did. I made the clever decision to only surround myself with grade A+ friends. But I kept them at an arm's distance. It probably didn't feel like that to them because I always made space for them and loved them hard. Always within my own parameters though. And I certainly didn't share the dark part of me. I held myself to such an unrealistic standard that it felt like admitting I needed help was akin to failing. So, I pretended. I pretended I knew what I was doing, and that I was okay.

It wasn't that I wasn't enjoying myself. I did have wonderful, heart-warming, belly-laugh, intimate and beautiful times. I had a beautiful partner who loved me unconditionally. I was smart, creative, optimistic and fun. But there was this pervasive tension behind everything. I think I had gotten so good at not acknowledging how I was feeling that I didn't even know that what I was feeling wasn't normal. I didn't know that there was another way to feel.

I had reached breaking point by the time I started to suspect ADHD. And, thankfully, I knew enough by then that it was time to face facts. Something had to change. For the first time ever, I allowed people to see the real me. I called my parents and bawled my eyes out with my suspicions. My parents did what they do best, which is fiercely supporting the fuck out of me. I broke down to my husband, and he did what he does best, which is hug me, support me and then take the piss out of me. I told a few close friends and was met with some incredulity but, ultimately, support. I told people so that I could lean on them, but I also told them so that I was accountable. I couldn't continue the way I had been. It was time to meet this thing head-on.

Pursuing the diagnosis

I made an appointment with my GP, Dr W, whom I love because she is kind, she listens, she is thorough, and she always makes me feel like she has all the time in the world for me. When I first moved to Perth I had a different doctor. When I would be waiting for that doctor to see me, I would see this beautiful, smiling woman come out to collect her patients. She always looked genuinely pleased to see them, and, somehow, I knew I could trust her.

I surreptitiously made enquiries about her name. I was also informed that she wasn't taking on new patients. I'm not above wilful suburban delinquency, so I took advantage of the recent introduction of online booking and booked with her anyway. I am aware that this is naughty, but what can I say? I'm a rebel. I was heavily pregnant with my second son when I arrived at that appointment. It didn't take the receptionist long to click that I wasn't one of Dr W's regular patients. She informed me that Dr W wouldn't be able to accept me as a patient, so I did what any about-to-pop pregnant woman would do. I cried. Sobbed would probably be a more accurate word.

The receptionist visibly sighed with displeasure but agreed to check with Dr W, and, sure enough, that kind soul took pity on me. Yes, I was in! It must have been serendipity because she has seen me through so many different things in my life now. Her unwavering support and ability to listen and thoroughly follow up has been a life saver.

I had been seeing her for over 7 years by the time I headed into my appointment to broach the subject of ADHD. I was feeling the impostor syndrome hard, but I went in with a comprehensive list of why I had come to have this suspicion. She listened and supported and confirmed that she thought it warranted further testing. She said she would spend some time trying to find a psychiatrist for me who specialised in adult ADHD. But I couldn't wait, so I did my own research and found Dr T. She passed on my referral, and I was placed on a 4-month waitlist.

It is worth noting here that not everyone goes through their initial meeting with their GP with such ease. I have seen many anecdotal stories about women who are dismissed, ignored and not listened to. Here are some of the crappy reasons I've heard general practitioners (and, more disturbingly, psychiatrists) give for why a woman should not pursue a diagnosis or further testing:

- ADHD doesn't exist.
- You're too old.
- You did well at school.
- It's just anxiety.
- It's depression.
- Everyone has struggles.
- People like you just want the drugs.

The last one makes me want to sock someone right in the solar plexus. Especially seeing as so many of us struggle to remember to take our medication. In fact,

I've forgotten if I *have* taken it and have been too scared to take another one in case I double-dosed. That's the hallmark of a drug addict – one who can't consistently remember to take it, or if they have taken it. Sarcasm intended.

ADHD is wildly underdiagnosed, particularly in women. Many women already find it hard enough to stand up and say, "I'm not okay, I need help." To get to the point where you reach out for assistance, and to then be shut down by ignorance is appalling. If this happens to you, I beg of you – *please* continue to seek help. You may have received a diagnosis of other mental health issues, such as generalised anxiety, bipolar or depression. Let me be clear, I'm not claiming that these diagnoses are wrong, but the rate at which I see stories of women who are misdiagnosed for years before finding out that they in fact have ADHD is alarming.

There are many doctors who are open to listening and honouring what you have to say. There are many psychiatrists who specialise in adult ADHD. And there are many psychiatrists who will listen to you. It's a fundamental right for people to have the correct diagnosis and medication, but perhaps most importantly for ADHD, it brings the chance to learn about how your brain works and why you do the things you do.

So, there I was on a 4-month waitlist. Patience ain't my forte, if you haven't realised by now. To occupy myself while I was waiting, I jumped into some serious googling. If you're reading this book because you suspect you have ADHD, or you've been diagnosed, you can probably understand the ferocity at which I threw myself into this. I was consumed. And I have never felt more seen.

I joined Facebook groups for ADHD women, worldwide and in Australia. I had the beautiful experience of learning just how accepting and supportive the neurodiverse community is. For the first time in my life, I was amongst my people. Their stories were my stories. I was finding out that many of the things I had done, felt or experienced were typical of ADHD. I had answers!

A word of advice for medical appointments – *always* ask to be put on the cancellation list. A few short weeks after registering with my psychiatrist, I was called and offered a cancellation appointment for the very next day. And that was it. I was in! I was elated. I knew that I was finally going to get some answers, and I felt so hopeful and excited. My husband was nervous. He wanted to protect me. He was worried that I wouldn't get the answers I was after.

I think we spend our whole lives fearing diagnoses. Generally, it doesn't carry a great connotation. Yet for me, the possibility of being given a diagnosis of ADHD was absolutely thrilling. At no time did I lament this. I couldn't wait to have it confirmed that I had what I suspected I had, so I could get on with the business of stepping into the next phase of my life.

My husband was concerned that the psychiatrist would tell me that it wasn't ADHD, and if it wasn't, my hope wouldn't just be shot – it would be annihilated. But in a volume of ways, I just *knew* I had ADHD. In all of the other ways, I was terrified that I was wrong.

The first appointment

I liked my psychiatrist, Dr T, as soon as I walked through the door. He exuded a warm dependability. I had performed a rigorous deep-dive on Google prior to the visit and had found that his website was specifically focused on adult ADHD. It was his compassionate approach to the subject that drew me to book with him. We chatted a little bit about why I was there, and, while I talked, he made notes. He assured me that he wasn't here to offer a one-size-fits-all solution.

He regards (rightly) each person as unique, with their own special needs, and that they should be treated as such. He believes in treating the whole person, not just one aspect. He ran through a series of diagnostic questions based around an ADHD diagnosis. He then asked me to fill out a form rating myself on a scale. (Adult ADHD report scales are readily available on the internet.)

I'm going to be honest here – I can't remember the whole appointment. That pesky working memory issue. I tend to remember moments, instead of details. I recall us discussing my symptoms and admitting that I was nervous at the thought of trying a stimulant due to being wracked with anxiety. I had read anecdotally that it can help with anxiety, but I had convinced myself that I would be the person who would experience the unfavourable side effect of making it worse. He looked at me kindly and promised he was going to look after me. And you know what? I believed him.

At the end of the appointment, he said that he was reasonably confident that I did in fact have ADHD. However, it was his procedure to send people away with a few things to collect before their official diagnosis. I walked out with a form for my parents to fill out about my childhood, one for Neil to fill out about the last 6 months and one for me to fill out. I also needed to find old school reports that may have any indicative comments. I had to have an ECG (an electrocardiogram, which records the electrical signal from your heart to check for different heart conditions as it's possible that stimulants aren't suitable for people with cardiovascular issues), a urine test and a blood test.

The only thing that worried me about my family and Neil filling out the forms was that I had been pretending how I felt for so long that I wasn't sure their answers would "be enough" to give an accurate picture of how much I had been struggling.

Then I remembered what Dr T had said. He had expressed that while it is interesting to him to see how others have perceived me, it's not the deciding factor. He takes into account many different things and listens mostly to me because I am the one who is experiencing the problem.

I stressed to my family and Neil that they should be honest and not bother with any sugar-coating because I wouldn't be offended. I couldn't keep living like this. Thankfully, they took my advice.

Apart from my mum on the question: Deliberately annoys people?

She answered, "Never or rarely".

Mum! Get the rose-coloured glasses off! I believe my brother would have something *very* different to say on that one, as I cast my mind back over memories of me pointing my finger at him, closely to his face, but not quite touching him and saying, "You can't get annoyed, I'm not actually touching you."

To be fair on Mum, she was supposed to think about my childhood, and I did that to him a few months ago as a full-grown adult.

Talks too much!

The irony of ADHD

It felt ironic to me – someone who had been struggling with "life admin" – to be asked to not only keep track of various forms, but to organise myself to get a multitude of tests done. Yes, it was 3 tests. No, I am not entirely sure what constitutes the use of the word multitude. Yes, I just went down a far-too-long wormhole looking up the definition of multitude. I'm still not 100 percent clear, so it's staying. Judge me if you will.

I need to stress how difficult it was for me to carry out these arduous tasks marauding as simple ones. The family questionnaires were easy. I printed them off at work for Neil and myself and emailed one to my mum and dad. I also asked Mum to hunt down my old school reports. We'd found them when I went back for a holiday not too long ago, so I knew they wouldn't be far.

Now I had to coordinate myself enough to get a blood test, a urine test and an ECG. I had been given 3 separate referral forms. I had 6 weeks to complete my mission, should I choose to accept it. Which is a problem because given too much time to carry something out, I WILL procrastinate until the last second. Amiright? Tell me you can't relate to that.

I guarded those forms with my life. Never have any forms been given the Kevin Costner level of bodyguarding that I gave those things. I had to carry them around in my backpack that I take to work each day because I couldn't trust myself to not leave them somewhere. They had to be in a plastic sleeve because I couldn't be trusted not to get my bag mysteriously wet somehow.

The handy thing was that I was working at a university with a pathology centre. So convenient! Off I went on my lunchbreak. Except it turns out that you need to take the forms your psychiatrist gave you to the appointment, not leave them snuggled safely in their plastic home in your backpack.

Take two.

Got to the pathology centre a second time. The phlebotomist started trying to take my blood. I would love to say that the "trying" part of that sentence was due to her incompetence; however, after a short moment she asked me how much water I had drunk that morning. My mind flitted over the zero drops of water I had drunk.

"Umm... a little bit?"

I figured if I said it like a question, she might take the reins and assure me that I had indeed drunk enough water.

"There's no blood coming out, you're too dehydrated."

The shame.

I'm joking – I didn't feel any shame. I did what I usually do, which is laugh at myself and feel pleased that I had a funny story to tell my husband, family, friends, work colleagues, the mail carrier, my kids' teacher... you get the drift. I had to leave, drink some water and come back. I also did something clever. *I left the referral form there.* Now it was her responsibility. Hah!

By the time I returned, I swam through the door, bursting at the seams with the gallons of water I had drunk. Blood flowed freely, and I had ticked one thing off.

The urine test had to be done at a particular pathology centre because they had to watch me wee. To make sure I wasn't weeing out of a fake penis and using a jar of smuggled-in urine perhaps? You laugh but apparently this happens, according to the wee-wee collection lady. But what I am glossing over is how long it took to get to this magical tinkle collector.

For starters, they only have the urine inspector there at certain times on certain days; information I found out far too close to my deadline to have any wriggle room with when I could go. I was also working full-time, so during the week was out as a possibility.

I like to do this thing that I will refer to later in the book as "Task stacking". I knew the collection place was close to where my kids play softball (I was the coach), so I decided to stack my tasks and pop in there on a Saturday morning before the game. *I'll get my piddle on and make it to the game with plenty of time to spare*, I thought. I had all the softball gear in the back of my car, so they couldn't play without me. I could see no potential issues here. Time blindness meant that I was a little behind schedule as I headed towards the pathology centre, but the softball field was only 10 minutes from there, so it would be fine.

Until I stepped through the door and saw a line of people snaking down the hallway. Clearly, they'd all had the same idea. It only occurred to me at *that very moment* that other people would have had the same problem as me trying to get there during the week and, of course, there were now 376 likeminded people lining up. The tragic irony of the situation I had found myself in, for the reason I was there, was not lost on me. After approximately 400 years, I was finally seen. I managed to wee on my hand (standard), but I was done. Another task finished! And I was only 30 minutes late to the pre-game warmup. Winning.

Out of all the things, the ECG was the easiest. I just carried that one out like I assume a neurotypical person would. I rang up, made an appointment, went there and had it done. ADHD likes to keep me guessing like that: "When will she easily carry out a task and therefore trigger her impostor syndrome? Stay tuned next week to find out!" Only, the catch is that you never find out. It's fun like that. But who cares – I had done it! And just in the nick of time before my follow-up appointment.

One last thing: for all those medical professionals out there who're reading this book, surely I'm not the only one who will most definitely choose a medical provider who allows appointments to be booked online? Actually, *any* provider – medical, hair, massage. If you have an online booking system, then I am 100 percent more likely to book through that than make a phone call. Just sayin'.

Congratulations – it's ADHD!

On the second appointment I entered proudly with my homework. I was so terrified that I'd lose the documents (likely) that I scanned them and emailed them to myself. I also ensured they never left my bag. But as I have learnt, sometimes I don't take my bag with me, so I had to set a reminder to make sure I packed my bag that day AND that the documents hadn't somehow jumped out of the bag and thrown themselves into the bin (also likely).

Dr T looked over the documents and was pleased to see that my family had been honest. He talked about how it's such a delicate process because parents don't always feel comfortable being upfront about their children, even if those children are 39 years old! It's possible you may feel hurt by your family or partner's answers. It might feel strange to ask people to essentially list all the weird stuff you've been doing your whole life, but I'm quite pragmatic about those kinds of things and saw it as them helping me get diagnosed. I was initially worried that they had scored me on the low side, such was my desire for Dr T to see what I was so desperately holding inside.

He gazed over my school reports that sung my praises academically, creatively and in the sporting arena, but with an overriding mention of my insatiable desire to talk my way through all my classes.

You know what? Let's stop for a moment and enjoy the comments from my school reports. The name of this book came from my drama teacher in high school, who said, "Alana is a strong performer. Good group skills. Talks too much!"

Here are some more for you to enjoy:

"So capable but distracted."

"Contributes well but can be distracted at times."

"Alana has a lot of ability, but she lets herself down by chatting when she shouldn't."

"Alana should pay close attention to verbal instructions."

My report when I was 6 years old says that I was achieving above averagely but that, "her social confidence can be overwhelming for her peers". That one makes me smile. I was strong, confident and LOUD. Still am.

Dr T looked at me kindly and said, "It's all there, isn't it?" No judgement though.

He then got me to sit a computer test involving shapes. The deal was that there were red circles, red squares, blue circles and, you guessed it, blue squares. They would appear on the screen in a random order. When there was a sequential occurrence of a blue square followed by a blue square, you had to press the space bar. He was explicit about not moving my head because the computer wouldn't be able to detect me. Or something. I tuned out for that bit. But I sat still.

It lasted 20 minutes and it was torturously monotonous. The thing is, I sit in front of a computer all day. AND I'm competitive. So, it wasn't hard for me to do the task. That's not the point though, is it? I'm *not* supposed to be able to do the task. So, I passed, which meant I failed. I passed on the lower scale compared to someone without ADHD, but a pass is pass and an ass is an ass.

Shit.

Luckily, once again Dr T reiterated his professional opinion that all these diagnostic tests form only part of the diagnosis. He noted that I spend my whole day in front of a computer, so it's likely that I've become conditioned to staring at a screen and reacting.

We sat back to discuss everything he had heard and seen from me. My bloods came back with low vitamin D, so it was decided that I would get a supplement, but also to make sure I got outside in the early morning and late afternoon to get some real vitamin D too. My drug screen came back clear – no idea how, I am a fiend for narcotics. Joke. It's a joke.

And he told me that it was his esteemed diagnosis that I did, in fact, have ADHD.

Well, duh. I didn't say that, I said, "I'm scared to try stimulants." And it was true. I knew the science behind how they worked, but just the word stimulant scared me. I was already so highly strung and felt like all it would take was a sliver of straw on the camel's back and I was going to be stark-raving mad. I had to trust him. I was apprehensive about trying them, but the thought of not trying and carrying on with no help was even more alarming.

Talks too much!

Reframing

Even prior to my diagnosis, when it became more and more apparent to me that I had ADHD, I began a process of reframing. It didn't take the diagnosis for this to start – as soon as I had my suspicions, I began to see things in a different light.

This is a typical process for people who are diagnosed later in life. I had lived a certain way, believing certain things about myself, and now I had the opportunity to go back and look at those experiences through a different lens. The overriding feeling I had with this process was sheer relief. It was like doing a puzzle that had been missing a piece and finally finding it where it had been kicked under the couch. It's possible that this process also brings up feelings of guilt, grief, anger and resentment.

I didn't feel any resentment. I was incredibly lucky as a child to have a family that embraced my individuality and loudness. I do recall being told to be quiet a lot, but I don't feel damaged by that. It certainly didn't work. I am still loud, make rude comments and try to distract people in meetings. I sound annoying but I promise I'm not. Okay, maybe I am, but you know what, take it or leave it, this is me!

I was curious about what the discovery of diagnosis meant for me, and I felt like I was sifting through my life gently making discoveries as I went. This is something that I still experience now as things pop up from my memories and I make a link to ADHD.

One of the biggest things for me has been the reframing of my anxiety. In the '80s and '90s it wasn't as widely recognised as it is now, but I was blessed with parents who were ahead of the game. One time, as an incredibly awkward 14 year old, I arrived at a friend's holiday house 3 hours out of my hometown. I found myself with my friend and her older siblings, who were all far cooler and worldlier than me. I felt incredibly uncomfortable. My body was telling me to GET OUT. I did what any kid would do; created a fake illness and called my parents, begging them to pick me up. And bless their little cotton socks, no questions asked, they jumped in the car straight away and made the 6-hour round trip to come and collect me.

Some people may look at that and think they should have left me. Teach me a bit of resilience. However, I can categorically tell you that this is one of the defining moments of my teenage-hood. From that moment forward I knew that if I needed a way out from a situation, they would come and collect me. If they had left me, I believe it would have been damaging. And guess what? I'm one of the most resilient people I know. Yes, that's right – you can be riddled with anxiety and still be resilient.

Over my younger years, I showed signs of anxiety, but I think I had my own ways of dealing with it, and I was free to use those tools to soothe myself. For example, after a bad breakup with my first boyfriend, I felt anxious around bedtime and getting to sleep. I would watch *Seinfeld* that a friend recorded on VHS tapes for me (it was the '90s, don't laugh) until I dropped off to sleep. Looking back, I can see that I had figured out a way to self-soothe. This can also be considered self-stimulating, which we will discuss more later. And, for the record, after starting medication and introducing a "no social media in bed" rule – I STILL watch *Seinfeld* every night before I go to sleep.

There is a process to reframing. A memory will pop into my head – it might be an event, or something I said, or a habit I have – and it will occur to me that maybe that situation or thing happened that way or I reacted like I did because I did in fact have ADHD without knowing it. There is a gentle shifting of my solid and set views on something.

I put myself back where I was. It's not hard because these were usually defining moments in my life. Then I gently explore around the idea of associating the memory with ADHD, feeling my way and testing the concept out. I can feel my beliefs shift and the new way of looking at it settles in.

Like many women, my perceived onset of adult anxiety was intrinsically linked to the birth of my first child. As I mentioned earlier, I went on to suffer panic attacks after my first son was born. For 12 years of my eldest son's life, I had linked my anxiety to parenthood and, as a result, in a way I linked it to him. I know that's not fair. But that is what happened.

I wonder how many women can empathise with this. If I reframe that experience through the ADHD lens, then I can hypothesise that perhaps I wasn't struggling with motherhood itself, but rather my way of coping was taken away. When it finally dawned on me that I might possibly perhaps just have a little bit of ADHD, this thought came to me:

What if becoming a mother wasn't what caused anxiety, but rather was the first time I could no longer use the coping mechanisms I had used my whole life to manage my ADHD?

B-FUCKING-OOM!

Right in the solar plexus. YES. Well, that's a whole different ballgame. I can detach those feelings of anxiety from being connected to my son. I can drop the shame. I can feel empathy and love for myself. It wasn't my fault. I'm not a shoddy mother. I was doing the best with what I had, and when I could do better, I did better. It is with so much time, deep diving and hard work that I can say those words. For so long I believed I was a bad mother, shrouding myself with shame and berating my behaviour.

> " *The feelings I assumed were anxiety related, were – most of the time – ADHD.* "

Every day since suspecting my diagnosis, I have started to become the kind of mum I wanted to be. I did not realise how much of my behaviour stemmed from shame. I knew there was something wrong, but I did not know what it was, so I just blamed myself. Why wasn't I like the other mums? How did they just know what to say and do? How come they could just back themselves and be so sure that what they were doing and saying was right? It turns out that my cute little brain just works differently to other people's. It turns out that I am more sensitive. It turns out that my first reaction was anger. Not because I was angry. Because I was terrified.

As this gradually dawned on me, I was able to start the slow process of gently challenging my definition of what I believed anxiety was within my body. I was beginning to understand that the feelings I assumed were anxiety related, were – most of the time – ADHD. I cannot possibly convey in mere words the significance of this discovery. This hypothesis was prior to starting medication, and was proved correct, as after I started medication, around 95 percent of my anxiety disappeared.

It's important for me to highlight that while my ADHD presents partly as inattentive type, it also presents as hyperactive type, most of which is internal. Yes, I can be quite loud when I'm in the right place, usually with my family or after several red wines with the girls. But the internal hyperactivity was what I was feeling and misinterpreting for anxiety. The cliché of a hyperactive child with ADHD jumping all over the place was living inside of me. And I judged that inner child, chastising myself for not being able to stop feeling and behaving that way.

I still occasionally get anxious. But when I get it now, it's situational. This means that something has happened to make me feel anxious – it might be a negative interaction with someone, or I might be feeling nervous. This form of anxiety is something that happens to almost everyone. Maybe it's not anxiety at all and it's just some good, old-fashioned nervousness. When my medication either hasn't kicked in, or it has worn off for the day, then the old feelings resurface. I know now that those feelings are not anxiety, they're untreated ADHD.

But the nameless, faceless tightness in my body, the ball in my stomach and the weight in my chest was being caused by a neurological disorder. I know now that my body was in constant fight or flight mode. My amygdala was over-performing (what a show-off) and relentlessly sending me messages that something was wrong. And

I was trying to feed it the story that I needed to be like everyone else.

I know now that without help I wasn't capable of being that person. It wasn't my fault. I had created a shame story around my perceived anxiety. I tried to ignore it, but its omnipresence would never leave me alone. I was beginning to see that my body had been trying to tell me a different story the whole time. I just could not slow down to hear it.

Now, with help, I set out on one of the most critical self-love journeys I had ever been on – intricately extricating a lifetime of memories and viewing them through an ADHD lens.

Looking back through the ADHD lens

As I have experienced the reframing of my past through an ADHD lens, I have also been able to recognise certain things that I know now were caused by or were a result of ADHD. I have been lucky in my outlook on life, where I can find the humour in most things. I've always considered myself an eternal optimist, and despite the many struggles I've shared, I am almost always able to find the funny side of things. I do wonder if my outlook would have been different if I had grown up knowing that I had ADHD. I wonder if I would have felt like how I dealt with things was wrong, or that I shouldn't have found them as funny as I did.

While I was incredibly critical of myself in many ways, in a total contradiction I also found myself incredibly entertaining. I can make myself laugh to the point of hysteria over the stupidest things, mostly things that I've done. Looking back on things I've always done in my home, work and family life, I know that they're probably different to what other people do, but I've never known why. Now I do. And I love going back and applying my knowledge of ADHD to things that have happened in the past.

I have always been able to entertain myself easily. I find myself far funnier than I find anyone else. It's not uncommon for my husband and me to get into a laughing fit over something, usually something silly I've said, and for him to leave the room, come back and find me still sitting on the couch silently laughing, with tears running down my face. I'm funny, okay?

I remember working somewhere where I needed to order more blinds. It was urgent, and as a result my brain decided that it would go blank and not be able to manage the burdensome task of finding the tape measure, going into the room and measuring the space, recording the details and then actually ordering the blinds.

At one stage, I found the tape measure and lost it again before I got to the measuring bit. I finally took the measurements but wrote them on a piece of paper and lost it. You're getting the theme here, right? BUT. Somehow, by some small miracle, I managed to coordinate all the tasks and order a huge 2.5-metre (8'2") blind. It did not occur to me to question why that custom-made blind was only $50. What a bargain. My friends, the image opposite is what turned up.

Turns out, I'd ordered a 25 *centimetre* (8") blind. It would have made a caravan owner very happy. It belonged in an incredibly boujee cubby. As you can see in the image, I am wildly entertained by my mistake. I am literally crying big happy tears in this photo.

I never did order the proper blind before I left for my next job. And you know why? Because despite the fact I found it hilarious, I hid the mistake from my boss. I couldn't bear to admit that I had caused yet another delay with the ordering of the blind. See, she had asked

me multiple times over multiple weeks to get it done, and I had procrastinated so many times that it was starting to get embarrassing, and I was starting to run out of excuses.

Now I know that the reason I found this task so overwhelming was because I had undiagnosed ADHD. It wasn't that I was being lazy or stupid. I have a neurological disorder that means I'm kinda crap at the skills required to carry out this task – organisation, time management, accuracy and paying attention. Luckily, I am also obviously able to laugh at myself. But behind the laughter was a bewilderment that what seemed like such an easy task was actually very difficult for me.

We've all seen this meme, right? Most people see this and have a little laugh. I saw this and thought, "Genius!" And then made myself the same sign. My reaction to someone who came to talk to me while I was working was one of two things – either I would push my chair back and eagerly turn towards the person, just waiting for whatever they had to offer me, distraction wise, or I would respond negatively because it took so much effort to concentrate that a distraction would make it so hard to get back into the groove.

My answer was this sign. The job I was in at the time meant I was the "hub" of a busy place. I had so many people who needed something from me that it was like someone with undiagnosed ADHD's dream and equally a nightmare. But it worked. Until I lost the sign and couldn't be bothered making another one. Typical.

While I was in the same role, we received deliveries that had to be opened, sorted then distributed to other rooms in the building. I couldn't do it. I knew I had to, and I knew it was simple. But I just could not bring myself to do it. It was like I had a blind spot. I knew the task was in my periphery and that it existed, in theory, but carrying it out was insurmountable.

The thing is, I love opening packages – who doesn't? But I knew that once I opened them, I would have to take them around to the various people who'd ordered them, and that was where I drew the line. With seemingly simple tasks like this, I developed a mental block. I knew it was there, and I knew I was supposed to be doing it. It would hum in the background, growing bigger and bigger, more and more insistent. But I was stuck.

In another job role I had to collect the mail. I'm seeing a theme here. Apparently, I have an issue with mail. The mailboxes were upstairs, and it was stipulated that I should collect the mail daily.

I did it approximately 7 times over my 12-month contract.

The mailboxes were out of my vision; therefore, they did not exist. Did I set reminders to do this task? Yes. Did I pay attention to the reminders? No. If by some miracle I did collect the mail, I would bring it back to my desk. The next tangible step would be to walk 2 metres and put it on my boss's desk. I would procrastinate over this one simple thing for days. The letter would sit there, positively throbbing with self-importance, and I would simply behave as though it didn't exist. When I finally did take the letter to him, it would take me all of 14 seconds. The relief of not having this unconquerable task hanging over me anymore was so wonderful.

Would it make me do the task quicker next time? No. I think part of the problem was that I knew the letters were not urgent. My brain decided not urgent = leave on desk for several years.

Even though I had difficulties at work, it felt like there was at least some order there because other people were running the place. At home that was my responsibility. And I wasn't excelling at it. I was just managing to hold it together, but there was a distinct lack of consistency. The cool thing is, now I know what was clouding everything, I can look back and know that there was a reason behind why things were the way they were. Funnily enough, some of these things still happen. The difference is that I now have a ~~excuse~~ reason.

I always found it kind of amusing that my whole family would quite happily step over something that had been left on the floor. I am talking *for weeks*. It could be a sock, a tea towel, even just a piece of paper. Eventually, someone would notice it and do something about it.

This has always been a source of amusement to me. I had no idea it was ADHD related. I can see the thing, and I know I should pick the thing up. But the task of *actually* picking it up is far too overwhelming. The thing doesn't bother any of us, it's just there. We all just step over it until eventually someone picks it up. Usually, the kids when I make them.

I honestly don't know how it is that I can spend an hour tidying and there be a new mess straight away. I would love to blame my kids, and yes, of course, they make mess too. But most of the time, I'm getting ready to confront my family over their slovenly ways and I realise it's ALL MY STUFF! I *swear* that there is another me following behind me so that as I'm tidying, the other me is making a different mess. Has it gotten better with medication? No.

I go through cycles with being tidy and messy.

That's a lie.

I go through cycles of being messy and less messy. The thing is, I prefer a tidy area. I work better, I feel better, and life seems to flow better. I just can't manage the bit where it stays tidy. If we had a bigger house and I had more money, then I would have a live-in housekeeper. Called Sven. Who was also a masseuse...

The only dedicated time I have to tidy the house is when no one else is home. So, picture this: I have the day to myself. My children are at their dad's, my husband is away for work and I have the house to myself. What I want to do is start the morning by cooking a yummy breakfast, then tidy up the house, take the dogs for a walk, do some writing and then just scroll mindlessly on my phone while ignoring a show I put on the TV, in my freshly tidied house. Note that I didn't say clean the house – that's just taking things too far.

But my brain does this thing where it invents things I "should" be doing instead. So, I'll say to myself that I should take the dogs for a walk before I do anything else. And seeing that I finally have the day to myself, I shouldn't use that time to tidy up. And I should read a book or watch a movie without picking up my phone. By that time, I have confused myself about what it is that I want to do, so I sit on the couch and feel paralysed by the choices. I would have been looking forward to this time for weeks, and now that it's here I am ruining it for myself.

Since my diagnosis, I have recognised that this trait is in fact due to ADHD. You may see it referred to as task paralysis. It's not that I don't want to do things, it's just that there is an invisible barrier in the way. I also attribute this to a lack of confidence in making my own decisions. I'm not entirely sure where I get the "I should" mentality from.

It may be partly influenced by social media, where I am constantly told that I should be aiming for more than just tidying my house on a free day. But guess what? I absolutely love having the time to tidy by myself with no one else around. I know it's not going to last but perhaps for at least one hour I can sit in a tidy house and feel like I kind of have my shit together. I'm also bombarded with the message that screen time = bad. But if being on my phone is what I want to do, then I can do that. My mum won't tell me off.

Now, with my new awareness I have freed myself up to make the decisions I want to make. For someone who is so disorderly and unorganised, I spend an inordinate amount of time tidying and organising. Not that it means I can ever find anything still, but for some reason it makes me happy. What can I say – I'm a messy, tidy, organised, disorganised person. I'm an enigma.

Another thing that I have realised is ADHD related is my fixation on certain foods. For several weeks I will make and eat, with relish, the same breakfast. It will taste just as good each time as it did the first time. I will somehow always make sure I have the ingredients to hand despite forgetting other essentials. And then, just like that, after weeks of loving that meal, I will take against it and will want to eat anything but that meal. I now know that this is a common trait of people with ADHD.

Similarly, I have always enjoyed songs way more if I can sing along with them. I will listen to them over and over until I know every word. I have since found out that this can be considered a form of auditory stimming.

Stimming is short for self-stimulation. It doesn't have to be the same song – I have a list of a few hundred songs that I have memorised. Considering the amount of music that has been made over my lifetime, to only have a few hundred that I will listen to is quite a small fraction. It takes a lot for me to add a song to that playlist. Within this playlist, I still struggle to listen to the whole song. Once the "main part" is over, I scroll to the next one. I need the stimulation of what my brain considers the best bits.

My lack of ability to listen to a song the whole way through probably explains why I struggle to sit through a whole TV show or movie without some sort of extra stimuli – in the form of talking the whole way through the any-thing I'm watching on the giggle box. This is something my immediate family has done my whole life, so it's always been quite normal for me. We like to pick apart the plot, take against people, guess the ending, etc. Writing this, I know that it sounds annoying. But, for us, it's how we enjoy the experience. The only time this doesn't happen is when the show or movie is exceptionally good. If that wasn't a big red flag for ADHD, then I don't know what is.

I am self-aware enough to know that not everyone talks their way through TV shows and movies, so when I first met my husband, I knew early on that he was the one. I had started from the first date being myself, so I wanted to continue that way. We were watching TV and I tentative-ly informed him that I talk the whole way through shows, and is that going to be a problem for him? He didn't even blink an eyelid, shrugged and said he didn't have an issue with it. I mean mainly it's not an issue because he seems to have some sort of compartment in his brain that filters out useless chatter. How else would he live with me (loud) and my neurodiverse kids (louder) and remain so calm?

Thankfully, his ability to roll with my quirks includes a blind spot for my talent of going off-task. Do you know what the best time is to start tasks you have been putting off for months, even years? You know, things like cleaning the oven or weather-proofing those shoes you've had forever? Well, according to ADHD, it's when I am already running late. Or when I am supposed to be doing anything other than that.

Never has this been more obvious than a few weeks prior to my diagnosis, where I found myself taking the oven door apart with a screwdriver and meticulously cleaning it – when I was supposed to be working from home. Or the morning I decided that it was exactly the right time to clean and tidy my bathroom drawer, despite the fact I had vowed I wanted to be early to work *and* the fact I hadn't even given this drawer one single thought for the past year.

Time blindness sounds negative. I'm going to refer to it as time optimism. My brain cannot tell how long things will take. Five minutes and 45 minutes can feel the same to me, and I am *always* optimistic that I can fit 732 tasks into the 10 minutes I have before I need to leave for the day. And I am always wrong.

Some part of me thought that being diagnosed with and medicated for ADHD would mean that I would suddenly be able to motivate myself to do certain things. That was not the case. Tasks are not necessarily easier to do if I don't want to do them. The medication clears my mind and makes it easier to focus but not always on the thing I should be doing.

Self-help for ADHD

One of the other fascinating parts of looking back on how I'd survived for the past 39 years was realising that there were so many tools I was using to help myself, without realising that the reason I needed them was because of ADHD. Reminders, alarms, stims and dopamine-seeking activities; I had always just done these things, but I didn't know why.

As I went through my life with a fine-toothed comb, many things stood out. Now I had a name and a reason why I did them. Obviously now, with hindsight, they are absolutely ADHD related. I just thought I was an absent-minded idiot with too much on her plate and in too much of a rush to get everything done. Obviously, that is still true, but now I have a neurological reason to blame it on.

First of all, can we have a quick chat about my love affair with my Apple smartwatch? It's a fantastic piece of technology with many wonderful and varied features. I feel that this is where someone on Instagram would say #notsponsored. However, should Apple be reading this – feel free to send a new one.

The number one feature is this: the watch has a little icon on the screen that you can press, and it will make your phone do a *ping*. And this is the important part; *even when it is on silent.*

EVEN WHEN IT'S ON SILENT!

For someone who never has their phone off silent, this is nothing short of a miracle. I have had my watch for 3 years and I have used this feature approximately 4,352 times. Probably more if I am honest. Did they make this just for ADHD people? It is glorious.

Most notable was the time I pinged my phone and the ping came from inside the washing machine. Yes, that's right, INSIDE the machine. While it was on. It was having a little surf in there, riding the waves and hanging ten. I'd been gathering bedsheets to wash (a rare occasion, like an eclipse – do not miss this rare sighting as it won't happen again for about 6 months), and, of course, I was carrying my phone.

In the 30 seconds it took to get to the washing machine, I forgot I was carrying my phone and it got chucked into the machine with the sheets. I appreciate my phone's dedication to still pinging even while on holiday to Hawaii. I am pleased to say that the combination of being able to open our machine while it is on, as well as it being a front-loader, meant that not only did the phone survive, it's still alive now. The rice thing does work. I had to go 2 days without my phone though – I am still scarred from that part and not ready to talk about it yet.

Thankfully, my phone survived because there's no way I can travel anywhere without it and its delightful maps. It doesn't matter if I've been somewhere 247 times, I can still get lost. I used to think it was just because I was forgetful. Now I know it's because my working memory isn't great. I just follow the map, which means I go on autopilot and don't pay attention to any milestones along the way. Occasionally, when I'm going somewhere I've been around 248 times, I start feeling bold and attempt to get there unaided.

I have this brilliant idea that I "should" know where I'm going. I drive, and, suddenly, I realise that I do not in fact have one single idea of how to get where I'm going. Looking around me, it dawns that I have somehow made my way into a foreign country. Even the street signs look like they're in another language. Sheepishly, I'll pull over and punch the address into Google Maps and note that I've managed to add an additional 13 minutes to the trip. Naturally, I do this on a day where I'm already running late. And when my petrol light has just come on.

I like to make things difficult for myself like that. I'm not entirely sure where the idea comes from that I "should know" how to get somewhere. Maybe from my internal narcissist who likes to attempt to trip me up every now and again. She's such a bitch.

It's not just external things that have helped me though. I have found comfort in my own body. Not that, get your mind out of the gutter. Okay, so sometimes it's that. Look, I'm not talking about that now – I'm talking about my hair! I have had long hair for most of my life. Apart from once, after I had my first son, when I decided that to be a proper mum you had to have short hair. I cut it all off, had immediate hair regret and proceeded to spend the next 3 years growing it all back.

The worst part about not having long hair was that I couldn't twirl it. I have done this for as long as I can remember, and once my hair was gone, it dawned on me for the first time just how much I liked doing it. The best is when my hair is freshly cleaned and straightened because the texture feels so comforting.

I know now that this behaviour is also stimming. Or, as mentioned, self-stimulation. Stimming is common in people with autism and can be common in people with ADHD. You may have seen someone rocking their body back and forth or flapping their hands. There can be more extreme forms of stimming such as head banging. Stimming is not always caused by distress. People can also stim when they are happy or bored.

For me, it is soothing and distracting. It gives my hands something to do and makes me feel good. It is dopamine inducing for me, and it can calm me down if I'm anxious. It is also a sensory thing – the hair feels nice in my hands, and it feels good at my scalp where the hair is being pulled slightly. I usually only do it at home, but if I'm comfortable, I'll do it in front of other people.

> ❝ *I struggle with activities where I am only doing one thing.* ❞

I do it when a conversation has gone on for too long and I am zoning out and need to entertain myself. Or if I'm feeling overloaded with the sensory input of an intense conversation, and I need to soothe myself. If we are chatting and I start twirling my hair, I'll just leave it up to you to figure out which one it is.

Another thing I have done for as long as I can recall is read in the shower. Yes, that's right. I take things made of paper into a little area that has spraying water. I remember when I was younger I used to hide this habit from friends and boyfriends. I would smuggle my books into the shower like a drug mule importing cocaine. My husband was the first partner I've ever been upfront with about my shower/book-reading habit. I have done it for as long as I can remember.

I do love to shower, but I struggle with activities where I am only doing one thing. That would sound so bizarre to someone neurotypical but so relatable to many people who are neurodiverse. The thought of having to stand in the shower and not have something else to stimulate my brain at the same time feels like torture. Other people may listen to music or watch stuff on their phones.

I've started being more open about quirks like this. The first thing people say is, "How does the book stay dry?" To be honest, it doesn't always. I have become adept at keeping it out of the spray but occasionally it gets wet. I am the kind of person who dog-ears their books, and I hold the wildly unpopular belief that a well-worn book is a well-loved book. I also tend to read the same books repeatedly, so they are bordering on being over-loved anyway.

Another time I must be reading is when I'm eating. The combination of eating and reading together is perfection to me. I have the fondest memories of being taken back to Mum and Dad's work after school, with a swing past the deli to get a packet of Burger Rings and a Coke. Mum would also let me go past the library where I would borrow the maximum number of books – 20.

Back at the office I was allowed to sit in the boardroom, eat and read. Even just thinking about it now makes me feel safe and warm and blissfully happy. Now I can recognise what I was doing back then. I was giving myself a dopamine boost; the double whammy. I would love to go back and give myself a huge high-five for being smart enough to create this infusion of dopamine.

I have so many memories of repeating this combination of reading and eating throughout my life. In fact, I don't have to cast my mind far because I did it this morning! Any chance I can, I make myself a delicious breakfast and a decaf coffee and I feel a visceral pull to read while consuming this feast.

Although that is like a red rag to a bull for my children, who see me sitting still (one of the only times in a day that I do) and want to talk to me. Nope. Nu-uh. This is Mum's dopamine-boosting time. Step away from the table! I won't move away until the alarm I have set to remind me that I need to be doing something else goes off, kids.

I could never figure out how people could just remember to do things. I couldn't grasp how people could have an appointment booked and remember that it was coming up. As technology has become more advanced, I have embraced every single organisational app out there. This means I download them and one of a few options happen: it's too hard to set up, so I never do; I use it obsessively for a few weeks then abandon it; or, it gets added to my sparse list of "things that stick".

The main loves of my life are Google Calendar, reminders and alarms. If you saw my colour-coded Google Calendar you could be forgiven for thinking I'm organised. It looks fantastic. But what you can't see is the dogged determination that was borne out of sheer necessity behind it. If it's not in my calendar, it simply does not exist. Sometimes it doesn't exist even if it *is* in there. That's why I also set reminders and several alarms for each thing.

Shortly before my diagnosis, I was walking back to my car with a work colleague one day. We would park away from our building so that we could talk and walk to and from work. Halfway back to my car, I realised I had left my smoothie behind. I wanted to go back and get it. It was going to be quicker to go to my car first and drive back to the office, so I set a reminder for 3 minutes' time to remind me to go back to the office, and then an actual alarm to go off for 2 minutes after that so I wouldn't forget that I had intended to go back to the office.

> *" My brain doesn't put things in order of importance. "*

She laughed warmly at my overzealous alarm system, but I knew it was necessary. Too many times I had intended to do something but as soon as I got in my car I went into autopilot and forgot. I had come up with this elaborate system as I knew it was the only way I could remember. My brain doesn't put things in order of importance. It goes, "We are in the car, let's drive home." I make accommodations to compensate.

Sometimes you need to set reminders about alarms and vice versa. And this is where my beautiful friend Siri comes into play. I know there are other versions for other phones, like Google Home or Alexa. Whatever it is, it is a gift from whomever God is to you. And if you're not using them then start. Now.

I tend to remember that I need to do things at times when I cannot use my phone. Mainly while I'm driving. But with a simple, "Hey Siri", I can get her to help me manage my life. I set reminders for EVERYTHING. Because I do not remember ANYTHING at a time that I am supposed to remember them. I have daily ongoing alarms for things like medication, and weekly ones for things like putting the bins out.

Here's a tip: never, ever turn off your alarm thinking you will then go and do the thing. You won't. Snooze the alarm but do not turn it off until the thing is done. I have snoozed an alarm for hours because I knew I wouldn't do the thing. And yes, I am aware I could have reset the alarm. But for whatever reason that was too overwhelming to manage so I kept snoozin'. Also, get yourself a reminder app that keeps the reminder on the screen until you choose to get rid of it. Trust me.

Sensory overload

I have spent my whole life feeling like I take everything "too seriously". I remember playing boardgames with my family and how much it pissed me off *to my core* when they didn't play by the rules.

One time we were playing Taboo. It's a game where there are playing cards and at the top of each card is a word. Then, under that word there are about 5 or 6 obvious describing words that you would normally use to get someone to guess the main word. However, the whole point of the game is to get your partner to guess the word/s at the top of the card *without* saying the ones underneath. It kind of goes without saying that you're not supposed to say the words at the top of the card either, right?

Well, my dad had a card, and the words at the top were "wedding dress". He was partnered with my brother. The clue he gave my brother was, "It's a dress you wear at a wedding." Obviously, you shouldn't use the words that the person is supposed to guess as a clue. As an adult, I can see the temptation to do that because it's kind of funny.

But at the time I was about 8, and I was FURIOUS. I was beyond ropeable. I couldn't understand why he couldn't just follow the rules, and, in my mind, he was cheating. It's fair to say that I lost my shit. I was subsequently banned from the game and the night was in tatters. And clearly it still annoys me because I can remember it so vividly so many years later.

This behaviour became an ongoing pattern for me. I seemed to feel things more than other people. I had a short fuse and was quick to take the bait every time someone laid some out for me. I couldn't really take jokes. I didn't (and still don't) like pranks. If someone pranked me, I felt like the person was trying to make me look stupid. I was loud and opinionated and passionate. About *everything*. It was exhausting. But I had no idea that I felt like that because I had a different brain. I was accustomed to being told to calm down and be quiet.

After having children, my short fuse grew even shorter. There was barely a fuse at all. I was so angry. Almost all the time. It wouldn't take much to push me over the limit. Usually, it was in reaction to something my children had done. I would end up having an adult meltdown where I would scream and cry, red in the face, and very much out of control. I knew I didn't want to behave like that, but something would happen, and I no longer had control. The shame afterwards was visceral. I wanted to do better but I couldn't.

I know now that my meltdowns were not because I was a bad person or a bad parent. I also know now that they were not actually caused by my children's behaviour. My brain and body were responding to an external stimulus, which would activate an internal response, and because I didn't have the ability to de-escalate, I would explode.

Prior to any inkling of ADHD, I had therapy with a wonderful psychologist, and she helped me process many things from my childhood that were causing me grief. It was so cathartic to leave behind many things that had plagued me for years, some I didn't even realise I was carting around. I was starting to shed some of the emotional weight I had been hauling around. While I was with my psychologist, I felt like a decent person, like I was capable of anything and that I could change my behaviour. So why, as soon as I was back home, did my resolve continually betray me?

> ✦✦ *Sensory overload doesn't always look like a meltdown.* ✦✦

Now that I'm medicated, I have enough clarity to answer that question. One of the reasons was sensory overload. Sensory overload is another condition that can be related to ADHD. As someone with ADHD I can't always decipher what information is important and needs my attention, and what information is superfluous and doesn't require my attention or my reaction.

I can be emotionally reactive, impulsive, not so great at self-regulation or monitoring and prone to hyperfocusing. This means I am reacting to a whole load of things, rather than the thing I am blaming it on – like my kids fighting with each other – particularly if I'm focusing on something that is giving me great pleasure and that requires my concentration. Being pulled away from that by the sound of bickering offspring is like fingernails down a chalkboard.

These behaviours meant I found it hard to figure out when I was approaching a feeling of "too much", and I couldn't decipher when I was about to reach the point of sensory overload.

Sensory overload can also be part of suffering from anxiety and can be brought on by being in situations that cause anxiousness. Sensory overload doesn't always look like a meltdown though. It can be felt in many ways, such as:

- irritability
- feeling uncomfortable
- panic attacks
- anxiety symptoms, such as quickened breathing, increased heartrate and sweating
- muscle tension
- headaches or migraines
- difficulty sleeping
- avoiding certain things
- over-sensitivity to certain things
- mood changes.

After my diagnosis, I began the slow process of learning about my triggers and how I would end up at the point of losing my shit. With the assistance of medication, I feel as though much of the internal stimulation I was experiencing has been eliminated. Because I'm not spending my days fighting an invisible beast inside of me, I feel more capable of identifying when I'm reaching the onset of sensory overload.

I find I can verbalise this a lot better now, and that by communicating how something is making me feel, I can cope with it better and not reach that point as much. I didn't realise how much I was keeping my feelings under lock and key, hiding what was happening inside of me.

Now I have the luxury of some spare room in my brain, and I can use that to choose more rational responses.

Please do not make the mistake of thinking this means that I've got it all together because I can categorically tell you that I don't. I still reach the point of sensory overload. But not as much as I did. And that's a win for me. I can now understand myself enough that I can communicate to the people who suffer the brunt of my sensory overload breaking point – my kids.

After it happens and the dust has settled, I can now approach them and explain the reason I got to that point. It allows my children to see that while I am not perfect, I am actively working on myself. This has the double effect of them being able to recognise these things in themselves, have names for them and see how they can try the same tools as me.

Talks too much!

Rejection sensitive dysphoria

As I mentioned earlier, one of the fabulous things about being diagnosed with something is that you can obsessively throw yourself headfirst into researching the absolute shit out of it.

I have found it enlightening to educate myself about me and why I have always acted or felt a certain way. When I discovered the term rejection sensitive dysphoria (RSD), it felt like a huge lightbulb went off. What I always thought was some personality flaw was an offshoot of ADHD!

Many people who have ADHD are also highly sensitive to what other people think or say about them. Or, like me, they are incredibly critical of themselves, and the sensitivity comes from what they think about themselves. RSD is not a medical diagnosis; it is just a way to describe these symptoms. The word "dysphoria" comes from a Greek word that means "hard to bear".

People who have RSD can become very upset if they believe someone has criticised them, even if it's not the case. RSD feels like an extreme version of insecurity, and can manifest as social anxiety, being easily embarrassed, taking things badly, ruminating excessively over situations, feeling rejected or having magnified reactions to situations that may not warrant such a response.

> ❝ *I was so sensitive to my own opinions of myself.* ❞

Pre-diagnosis, I struggled as a parent to make the many choices and decisions required. Because I was so jumbled inside my own brain, having to be responsible for other people was a crushing burden. My children would argue with each other and look to me for a solution, but I couldn't figure out who had done what, and which child I was supposed to be dealing with.

I would become so emotionally swamped that I would effectively melt down, yelling and losing control of my grip on my role. Tears would flow, along with the despair of not knowing how to make it better. I was fighting a battle inside of my brain, and the external stimulation of other people was just too much. My kids would retreat, shocked that their parent was acting that way. And as time went by, more sadly, they began to get used to it.

Later, I would feel such extreme culpability that I would lay in bed sobbing my eyes out, wracked with guilt. I was a terrible person. I believed I was ruining my children. For me, RSD was something I was doing to myself. I was so sensitive to my own opinions of myself. I was my biggest critic, my harshest reviewer. And it didn't matter who told me differently – only I knew the sobering truth.

I struggled with RSD at work too. If I received constructive feedback about something, I would take it as a criticism. I didn't want to be told what to do, even if their advice was right. I thought they would think I was an idiot if I made even the slightest mistake, so I would lie and cover up errors. I would pretend that I'd heard instructions even though I hadn't. And there was no way I was going to go back and clarify with a question. In my eyes that was akin to failure.

I always felt as though I needed to have clarification ready for things, just in case someone challenged me on something. I didn't know how to ask for help because I didn't know I needed it.

I played a lot of sport as a child and young adult. During a game, if I made an error, I would beat myself up about it. I was so mortified that I had done something so stupid. Why was I like this? It wasn't hard to play well. I conveniently ignored the fact that other people were making mistakes too. Their mistakes didn't seem as bad as mine, I would tell myself. In fact, I was understanding of their errors and was quick to reassure them. I wanted to be perfect, even though cerebrally I knew that wasn't possible. And when I was flawed, I gave myself hell. I can still rattle off multiple things that I did in games many years ago that were wrong, but I couldn't tell you a thing about a mistake anyone else made.

As a result, I would play the game from my head, already pre-berating myself about the mistake I was going to make. This meant that I made more mistakes than I would have because of the extreme pressure I placed on myself. Now when I coach, I can see the kids who feel like I did, and I tell them, "You're playing from here," while pointing to my head, "try playing from here," while pointing to my heart. Doing anything from the heart adds a good 38 percent* to the chance of success.

---

* Completely made-up number.

Many people with ADHD care deeply about what other people think. And, as a result, we work hard to ensure that everyone likes and admires us. This can present as us "masking", meaning we seek to hide or minimise our ADHD traits to fit into the neurotypical world.

The problem with masking is that there is almost always a fallout. For me, masking contributed to my feeling of being constantly anxious, wound up like a spring. You've heard of a jack-in-the-box? It's usually a metal box with a handle on the side. You wind the handle and music plays. After a certain number of turns, the top flings open and out pops a clown. That was me – slowly being wound up until the inevitable pop. Only my pop wasn't a fun surprise.

People with ADHD struggle to fit into a neurotypical world because we are constantly being told that our way of doing things is wrong. We get messages from a young age that we upset people with our behaviour. No one wants to be in trouble, let alone being in trouble for just being ourselves. So, we try to do things differently, but doing it that way feels uncomfortable. It feels as though everyone else is operating from an instruction book that wasn't made available to us.

Our body is giving us messages that this is not right for us, but we look around and everyone else is doing it that way, so we persist. Other neurodiverse people are doing the same thing so there is no example to base our normal on. We are giving ourselves an internal message that we are essentially "wrong", so when someone else says something even mildly critical, we hear it as a huge insult. Our own sense of self is already in tatters, so this unwelcome feedback is magnified.

RSD can affect every part of your life. From romantic relationships to friendships, to your family life and your work life. Being a sensitive person can be hard work. As women with ADHD, we often feel like we are always waiting to receive criticism. Travelling along hand in hand with impostor syndrome, we spend our lives expecting that our failures – perceived or not – will be found out and we will be rejected. It is widely acknowledged that women already have lower self-esteem and less confidence, so adding RSD on top of that can be crushing.

I used to really struggle with expressing myself when something had upset me. As a child, I wasn't always allowed to express my emotions, or I was met with a poor reaction when I did so. Because I was made to feel as though I was "too much", it meant that I spent my life trying to be "just the right amount". Now, with my newfound wisdom and a healthy dose of retrospect, I wonder if my parents were also suffering from sensory overload and struggled to deal with my big emotions. After all, I'm not perfect, so there was no way for them to be either.

As a young adult, I chose relationships that were not healthy for me, and I behaved in ways that were not true to myself. I believed that my authentic self wasn't good enough, so I pretended to be someone else. I also accepted behaviours from partners that were not healthy. When I was criticised, I believed it. It just cemented the feelings I was already having about myself.

When I tried to bring up things that upset me, my ex-partner would retaliate, and I would become confused about the point I had been making. My working memory was lacking (not that I knew that at the time), so I would get jumbled up and not able to finish the conversation. I would be railroaded into the whole thing being turned around and it being my fault. I'm not sure if it's a coincidence, but I see a high rate of stories from women with ADHD who end up in relationships with narcissists.

As an adult, there have been situations where I've felt as though the person I am dealing with has been rude or unfair to me. Previously, this would mean that for all intents and purposes I would basically write this person off and not want to have anything to do with them. My perception of the conversation was often far more exaggerated than what had really taken place. I don't know about you, but I spent my whole life reacting badly to certain situations, and because I was hurt and angry, I would cry and then shut down. If I could avoid the person I would.

I had a chance not long after my diagnosis to view my reactions through a different level of understanding of myself and how my brain works. A colleague said something in a meeting that really upset me. I went away and did have a little cry about it, but then I decided that this was the time I was going to deal with it differently. Instead of hiding away, I started a conversation with her about it. I realised that my understanding of the situation was limited because I hadn't asked for further clarification, so I was basing my feelings on a LOT of assumptions and, quite honestly, things I made up inside my own head.

My perception was different from the reality. This is classic RSD. I was so proud of myself for pushing against what RSD was telling me and to have a conversation instead of cutting this person off.

For me, it's partly a trust issue. Because I have been hurt by people before, I often feel like I'm waiting for the other shoe to drop. Trust, to me, means that people always stay the same towards me. It doesn't mean that I don't want them to have their own feelings and emotions, it's just that when they do have those emotions, I can't handle it if they're turned onto me. If someone is sad, or angry, or needs help, then I am your girl. But if someone is hurt and sad and angry about something that has nothing to do with me, but they're rude or mean to me as a result, then my trust is broken.

Consistency equals trust. The saying "What you see is what you get" is something I seek out in people, and it's what I offer in return. I see my relationships with those around me as connections. These grow over time and strengthen as we share experiences with each other. When someone breaks my trust, I feel it badly.

Knowing that it's part of RSD, or ADHD, or being a sensitive person doesn't make it hurt any less. But what it does do is allow me to process and compartmentalise those feelings. In those times, I draw my support from the consistent people in my life, and I lean into their benevolence to allow me to "make it into a bubble and blow it away". The positive news is that being aware of these things is a *huge* leap in the right direction. Examining a behaviour that no longer serves you, and being able to work on it, is hard. But it's not impossible.

Now that I am aware that I have ADHD and suffer from RSD, I have been able to make inroads into learning more about myself and understanding why my brain works the way it does. Having this insight prompted me to look back on experiences I've had in my life and examine them through a different lens. The behaviours that I thought were "wrong" were caused by something, not just me being a crap human.

Talks too much!

Dopamine seeking

Another discovery I made post-diagnosis is the term "dopamine seeking". I know now that many behaviours I've displayed over my life were related to the lack of dopamine my body naturally produced and the desire to create my own.

I had no idea that was why I did them. I just did them because they could incite feel-good feelings. Now that I understand how my body and brain work a lot better, I can do those things on purpose. I can recognise when I am suffering from feelings of low dopamine. As I will discuss later, we know that dopamine is a hormone and neurotransmitter that makes us feel good. People with ADHD naturally produce lower levels of dopamine than people without ADHD.

Pre-diagnosis, one of the ways I found to boost my dopamine was scrolling on social media over and over and over. I would lay in bed, trying to quell this feeling I had inside of me, but I never got to the point where I felt satisfied. So, I would keep going in the hope that the next video I saw would be the one that would make me want to go to sleep. I would also scroll on my phone while watching TV. Interestingly (and probably annoyingly), I can scroll on my phone and watch TV at the same time, but if my husband does it, I proclaim that he's being "too distracting!" Pot, kettle – you know the saying.

I have since realised that what I was doing was dopamine seeking. I was trying desperately to satisfy something inside of me that needed to be sated. When my husband is home, it's easy to get into bed because I have someone to talk to and hold hands with. My dopamine is being activated by his presence. Without him, I'm like a flailing idiot in the ocean trying to grab onto anything that goes past. Particularly those videos about dogs that get rescued and their transformations. Awwww.

Runs off to find one of those videos.

I came to the realisation that social media is a bottomless pit and there is no "end point" to it. I needed to create my own end point. And the thing is, I am always changing the end point because that's the way my brain works.

For a while I would crochet before bed. I could do this while watching TV and it would create enough dopamine for me to feel good. It meant that my dopamine bucket was being filled and I no longer needed to scroll in bed. Making granny squares was perfect because the end point was obvious. I had achieved something. It didn't matter how small.

Another tactic that works for me is going back to my teenage trick of watching *Seinfeld* re-runs. I do this while playing a game that is supposed to be for children. Now, here is the trick. I only EVER watch *Seinfeld* just before I go to sleep. I feel like I have trained my brain to feel happy about going to bed because I get to watch *Seinfeld*, and I associate my favourite show with sleepy time, eliciting a sleep mode that allows me to drift off easily. No offence to Jerry Seinfeld, of course. There is also a point in the game I play where I run out of lives. So now, no more lives = sleep. Sometimes I don't even make it to that point, and I go to sleep earlier.

Another trick I use is to always have something to look forward to. Once I close my eyes, I start to think about the "thing". It can be my kids' birthdays, so I think about what I'm going to buy them. It also works for Christmas. Before I got married it was thinking about the wedding. It could be a holiday, a weekend, an outfit you want to buy or your latest crush. Or your latest hyperfocus. It could be whatever your heart desires. I lie there and think about that thing, creating my own little dopamine fest inside my head, until I drift off.

The thing is, though, there is a limit to how much dopamine I can create on my own. I am up against the physical restriction of my body's ability to make it. It turns out that I need more help than a familiar TV show and some crochet. I need help of the pharmaceutical type.

Talks too much!

Medication

This chapter mentions stimulant medication. It is my intention to share my and my family's story as an anecdotal example of our experience. This is not medical advice. You should always seek the advice of a medical professional for advice, diagnosis and treatment. Never disregard professional medical advice or delay in seeking it because of something you have read in this book.

Let's just start off by saying that I am (obviously) not a medical professional. It's up to you to pursue your own diagnosis and, if you want to, take medication. My experience will possibly be vastly unlike yours. Each person in this world has their own set of life happenings, chemical makeup, physicality and way of dealing with things.

As I mentioned earlier, I was quite frightened by the thought of medication. Because of my history with anxiety, I couldn't quite grasp how a stimulant could do anything other than make that worse. I did lots of googling and read many personal recollections from the groups on social media. I was slightly hesitant about putting too much importance on anecdotal stories because I knew that so many other factors affect the outcome. But still, it was reassuring to read success stories and helpful to read tips people had found useful in the management of their medication side-effects.

After my diagnosis, and prior to medication, I had an immediate improvement with what I thought were anxiety symptoms. I found that having a name for the way I'd been feeling was gratifying. It was a relief when I found myself being nicer to me. It meant I was being kinder to my kids. The knock-on effect was an alleviation of shame. Despite this, I still had the feeling of almost always having a heavy, tight chest.

Years before ADHD was a consideration, and I first saw my psychologist (not to be confused with my psychiatrist), she would ask me where I was feeling my tension. She suggested that perhaps, as I was having trouble with my communication, it was in my throat. But it was always my chest. I had long endured a deadweight feeling permanently compressing my chest. To alleviate the pressure on my chest, I would repeatedly attempt to take in a colossal breath of air, trying to fill my deflated chest. I would expel air noisily out of my mouth, but the heaviness persisted.

The first day I took medication it went away.

The night before I tried medication I didn't sleep well. I tossed and turned, super aware of what the morning would bring. I thought there was no way it was going to help me. I imagined myself having panic attacks. I had to console myself with the thought that I knew it would be out of my system by the end of the day. I told myself that if I didn't like it then I would just stop taking it. Maybe I was wrong, and I didn't have ADHD. Did I trick my psychiatrist? Maybe I would be someone who reacts badly. Pretty positive thoughts, right? I couldn't let myself imagine that it would help. Despite, oh you know, years and years of medical research showing that it could.

In the morning, I took the first capsule and sat down and did some writing. The medication I was prescribed was a long-acting lisdexamphetamine. After 2 hours I could feel the beginning of *something*. It was subtle but because it was something different it made me consider feeling nervous. Despite the wintry weather, I grabbed my dogs and took them for a walk in the woods near my house, where I could let them off the lead. They were having the time of their lives while I battled gale-force winds and slashing rain. But never mind that – everything was so CLEAR. The world looked so crisp and bright. Was *this* something? Or was I just imagining it?

Gradually, a feeling of wellbeing came over me. What was it? I did a quick body check and let out a sob. There was no tension in my chest. My chest rose and fell softly. I didn't need to gulp in deep breaths of air. I stood in the woods, closed my eyes and let the tears fall. At which point both of my dogs decided to do a simultaneous poo, so I had to stop crying and take a photo and send it to my husband who was working away. What? Don't judge us.

" *What I believed was anxiety was instead the feeling of untreated ADHD.* "

As I walked on, I listened to an audiobook and I noticed something unusual. I was only listening. I wasn't listening and having my mind wander off onto 435 different tangents. *I was just listening.* Later, after I had returned from my walk, I felt like cleaning the house. We need to all take a knee right now and appreciate this for the miracle that it is. Not only did I feel like cleaning, but I dealt with the piles of crap I had lying around my house

127

that I normally felt too overwhelmed to deal with. I started tidying an area and I finished tidying the area. Okay, so I did have to remind myself to come back sometimes when I wandered off, but, on the majority, I finished what I started. I didn't get derailed by distractions.

I went to get my nails done and watched a highly educational show on Netflix while they were being done. Okay, shut up, it was *Love Island*. And I noticed that I was WATCHING *Love Island*. Like, not sitting there with one ear and one eye on the show while stressing that she was doing my nails right, and what was that lady over there doing, and ooh look at that, and listening in to other people's conversations. I was just watching. I was paying attention. Yes, it was trash, and yes, it was lowering my IQ by the moment, but that's not the point. I was focused. She didn't need to remind me to relax because I already was.

For the rest of the day, I revelled in my newfound skills. I felt slightly sad for my past self. I couldn't believe I had made it to 39 years old before I sought help. This difference between the previous day me and today me was palpable. Being free from my internal tension allowed me to truly admit how hard things had been. I did feel slightly "buzzy", but I was told that this would settle over time.

After all, this was my body's first experience with a stimulant medication. The medication started wearing off around 5pm. It was subtle at first, and then by around 8pm I felt tired. And along with it wearing off came my old feelings. I felt flat and worried. My brain was telling me that I didn't think I should have the medication the next day. I'm not sure on the logic of this, but it's what went through my head so I'm going to be honest about it.

Months on and the medication has continued to bring me a sense of peace. I have paid attention to my body and marvelled in the feeling of ease in my chest. It took a few weeks of adjustments, particularly as I titrated up my dosage on my psychiatrist's recommendation. I did feel a sense of being "revved up" at the beginning, which seemed natural as my body was adjusting to never having had stimulants before. I knew that this was not the aim though, so when that feeling began to settle, I felt more comfortable.

I read somewhere that the aim of stimulant medication is to not feel them working. At first, I couldn't fathom how that was a positive thing. But now I get it. When my dosage is correct, I don't feel any less myself or like I'm a different person. It doesn't dull my personality or change me in a negative way. I still do ADHD things. It's not a cure. I know that they are working because I feel indescribably better. But they work in a way that makes me feel what I imagined "normal" felt like. I'm me, but free within.

What I believed was anxiety was instead the feeling of untreated ADHD. It's no wonder we see children with ADHD unable to sit still. I can now empathise with that feeling of needing to move to rid yourself of the build-up of feelings inside. Add being too young to understand what is happening to you, it's no wonder that children feel out of control.

Something that was a total revelation to me was that I still have ADHD. Duh, right? Well, it didn't cross my mind until I'd started the medication. I had spent so much time worrying about what could go wrong that I forgot to think about what would happen if it went right. In the back, far reaches of my mind, I guess I knew that I would still have a lot of the struggles that I did before. I supposed I hoped the medication would make me more interested in the work I didn't want to do. It doesn't. I still have a brain that is interest-based. I probably thought I would get to places on time. I don't.

Over time, I have come to see that being on medication doesn't mean I never get sad or upset. I still feel all the emotions that I always felt but the prevalent heaviness has gone.

I still get annoyed when my kids spread mud all over the CLEAN BATHROOM FLOOR. I do feel I have grounds for my annoyance on this one... I probably clean the bathroom floor once every 6 months. Go on, judge me. I'll be over here pursuing dopamine-boosting activities instead. But I don't buy into every single one of my kids' arguments anymore either. Previously, the sound of the kids fighting was like fingernails down the chalkboard, but sometimes now I don't even register that they're having an argument. And guess what? Sometimes they manage to deal with it without my intervention. Miracle.

While I still struggled with my memory, organisation and time management, the pervasive struggle that had been clouding everything was gone. To not feel constantly anxious is absolutely life-changing. I feel like I've been freed from a prison I didn't realise I was in. The heavy feeling I'd been carrying around was lifted. Suddenly, life seemed that much easier. At first it felt scary to trust feeling good. It sounds crazy as all we ever want is to feel happy. I felt happy, but I was worried about relying on it. I hadn't felt like this before, and I didn't want to let it go.

There have been so many positives. I started smiling at strangers. I can't possibly tell you how much of a revelation this was for me. I was usually so awkward that I pretended to be on my phone if I was walking towards someone in the corridor. If I ever caught eyes with them, I looked away immediately because it felt so uncomfortable to me. Like, how many seconds do we hold eye contact for? What if they want to talk to me? Ugh! Now, instead of hiding from extreme awkwardness, I am that person who holds people's eyes and smiles. I will say hello! I'm the weird person who will start a conversation when we are trapped in the lift together.

Another thing that changed for me was my openness to being taught life skills. As an example, previously I was unhappy with my parenting. I knew there were plenty of courses, or advice, out there. I didn't want to know it. I knew it helped other people, but for me it felt like just one more thing I had to take into account. It wasn't that I didn't want the help or appreciate that there were plenty of people who were experts, and I could learn from them, I just simply could not process one more thing.

I was overwhelmed by basic life and that was my limit. After medication, I felt receptive to learning, welcoming of new perspectives and ideas. My mind has been expanded on so many different topics. I have a particular interest in ADHD, of course, and learning about my children and how I can be the best parent for them, so that they can be the best version of themselves. By removing the constant weight I had on my shoulders, I've been set free.

Now I can ask for help and appreciate what others have to offer.

I don't feel angry much anymore. I was so used to listening to my internal narcissist, who was all too ready to tell me where I had messed up. She's gone quiet now. Sometimes she tries to come back; at night, when the medication has worn off and my defences are down. But I can face her now, safe in the knowledge that tomorrow I can take my medication and she will be banished where she belongs. I am eternally grateful that I can have medication every day.

Over time I have experimented with what time I should take my medication and what I should eat with it. At first, I was so nervous about it affecting my sleep that I took it at 5.30am to ensure it was out of my system by the end of the day. I have adjusted that, and it works best for me to take it at 8am so it kicks in for when I start work. You might find that having it earlier helps you through that morning madness of trying to get out the door on time.

I tried caffeine and no caffeine. Caffeine pushed me past the point of calm and made me anxious again. So now it's the decaf life for me. No regrets – I would take how the medication makes me feel over anything. I find that eating food before I take my medication means that it comes on more subtly and lasts longer in the day. I try to take my medication after eating protein, and not on an empty stomach.

Having my medication on an empty stomach had adverse effects for me. I went up a dose (on a titration plan from Dr T) without eating first and found myself shortly after cleaning the shower with a toothbrush. I have quite literally never had that urge before! The medication hit me hard, and I was buzzy. It was kind of fun, but it wasn't a long-term feeling I wanted to have.

If you've noticed that your medication isn't working as well as you'd like, it's worth looking at your diet and checking how much citric acid you are consuming around the same time as your medication as it can affect the absorption of stimulants. Before, and until you can feel the effects of the medication, it's best to avoid things like juices, soft drink, muesli bars (or anything that can sit in a packet for months without going stale – it's sure to have high levels of preservatives like citric acid), high-vitamin cereals and vitamin C supplements.

My psychiatrist also recommended that I eat lots of protein. For me, protein helps with a more gradual absorption of the medication. Now that I eat a protein-rich breakfast, I can feel that my medication is steadier, and I don't have the drop off in the afternoon.

Talks too much!

High school

Now that my mind was clearer, I could look back on my life and recognise times where I unknowingly struggled. The first time I remember having an issue was as a teenager, when life had started filling with more responsibility, and the ball that I had kept so high up until then was starting to drop.

I can now see that my ADHD struggles were coming to the surface in my final year at school. I didn't know it at the time, and, as is typical, I blamed myself for "slacking off". As I mentioned earlier, I didn't struggle at school academically. The only subjects I struggled in were the ones I was either not interested in or I didn't have a connection with the teacher.

Throughout my schooling, I remember the teachers I loved, who accepted and supported me. And I tried to forget those who did not. When I collected my old school reports to share with my psychiatrist, there was a recurring theme. I shared some in that chapter, but here are some more for your amusement:

"Keen but talkative."

"Alana shows above average ability but at times is too talkative."

"Very enthusiastic. Can chatter about work – this can distract others."

"Behaviour usually good but can be drawn into inappropriate behaviour on unnecessary occasions." (I have questions about this one – were there times when inappropriate behaviour was necessary?)

"Periods of unsettled behaviour in class. Needs to be more consistent."

"If you're spending time being silly, you cannot be working to potential."

I don't recall being shamed for these comments on my report cards. Perhaps my parents made noises about how I should try harder, but it's not a memory that sticks. After my diagnosis, my mum started thinking about the possibility of her own potential ADHD diagnosis. She got her school reports out and I'll let you take a guess at what the comments were. When I was getting these comments as a child, chances are she was thinking about how she too had the same ones.

I have heard many anecdotes from women who've been told that they cannot possibly have ADHD because they did (and continue to do) well academically. This is categorically untrue. It is possible to be highly intelligent and have ADHD. Not only is it possible, but it can also be common for these women to have a high IQ. Misinformation is still quite common around this misconception. It is why I urge people to pursue a diagnosis with someone who specialises in adult ADHD.

Fun fact: if you have a high IQ and ADHD, you are what is called "twice exceptional". It's true – look it up. I don't even know what my IQ is, but I'm just going to assume it's high, and therefore I am twice exceptional. I never promised you facts in this book.

As I got further into my schooling, the work began to get harder. What worked in my favour was that the school allowed you to choose electives, and I was lucky enough to have parents who supported my desire to choose subjects I loved. I distinctly remember saying to them that in my final year I wanted to pick subjects I really liked because *that was the only way I was going to do the work.* Keep in mind that I was a kid who had cruised through school to this point – I mostly achieved As, with the occasional B. But somehow I intrinsically knew that to get through my final year, I had to be engaged.

I find it so interesting that I was self-aware enough at that age to say that was what I wanted and what I knew would work for me. And I am also giving my parents a virtual historical high-five for being progressive before their time.

I chose English, art, drama, outdoor education and mathematics. Mathematics was chosen purely because there were rules around how many "fun" subjects you could do compared to the boring ones. Okay, so maybe that is my interpretation, but you get the gist.

Despite being allowed to self-direct my choices, I began to disengage. I wrote and signed sick notes from my mum with a varying array of excuses as to why I had to leave school and then called my boyfriend to see if he was home. Off I would hop in my Mitsubishi Sigma and drive to his house to make out with him for the rest of the afternoon.

This was when mobile phones were only just coming out. My dad gave me an old one of his, which I used so rarely that I left it in the glovebox when I wasn't using it. I wouldn't keep it on, only firing it up when I needed to make a phone call. It had removable and interchangeable batteries, including a thicker one that lasted longer. There was only a tiny screen, and you couldn't save phone numbers in it. No one else had a mobile phone so I just had to remember everyone's landlines. It is official, I am old.

It's hard to say if my boyfriend (and my raging hormones) were the reason I lost interest in school. Or if, in retrospect, it was overwhelm from having to manage a much larger workload than I'd ever had before. I have such a clear memory of trying to memorise facts for my art exam and producing the plan of creating complicated acronyms to try to get anything to stick in my head.

I knew the curriculum. I just couldn't stop the details from slithering back out of my head every time I had to recall them. I would read them again, acknowledge to myself that yes, I remember that fact now, go to translate it onto paper and pssssshhhttt – out they all went from my head, always staying just out of my grasp.

Somehow, despite this, I ended up with a tertiary entrance rank of 81.5%. I know, without a shadow of a doubt, that I was capable of more. I have spent my whole life casually putting it down to my disinterest in schoolwork and a huge interest in rolling around in my boyfriend's single bed behind our parents' backs.

But what if, *what if,* I did not do as well as I could have because ADHD was impairing me, and I had no idea? This was 1999. There was no social media, no TikTok videos bringing awareness and information. There was no way in the world that ADHD would ever have been a consideration. It was generally accepted that I was a good student; however, I *did not try hard enough; Alana rushes her work; Alana talks too much; Alana should be more concerned with finishing her work than what others are doing in the classroom; Alana has so much potential, but she needs to concentrate more.*

What if I physically and mentally couldn't?

Looking back on this made me question how my children were moving through the school system. I had already spent a few years at this stage advocating for my eldest son for help with his auditory processing disorder. He had managed well, but by the time he hit high school, the wheels started to fall off. Was the fact that he was under much more pressure to blame? Or was something else at play? The school hadn't reported anything, but he was displaying an alarming level of anxiety. As his responsibilities multiplied, so did his reluctance to attend school.

I had seen firsthand the way my youngest son had benefited from being treated with anti-anxiety medication that wasn't a stimulant. But now he was showing signs of distress after school too. He reported feeling as though he wasn't achieving well, although his teachers said the opposite. I was all too familiar with this scenario – pretending you were fine on the outside, while crumbling on the inside. He was trying to tell me something. The message was being delivered in the form of overwhelmingly distressful meltdowns.

I don't mess around with mental health. If my kids are showing signs that they need help, then I will damn well get them help. I had suspicions that my eldest may have dyslexia, but I was also starting to wonder if he had inattentive ADHD too. I booked him in for assessments for both and was met with the issue that many other families face – a waitlist of 6 months for an ADHD assessment. As our awareness grows, so does our desire to get help for our kids, but the demand far outweighs the ability to manage it.

While we waited for his dyslexia assessment, I booked him in to see a psychologist and approached the school for help with his current diagnosis. To their credit, they came to the party and immediately put some methods in place to ease things for him. Feeling seen and supported is paramount to me.

Meanwhile, it was time to get more help for my little guy. Thankfully, he was already on the books of our wonderful paediatrician. I knew in my heart that it was time for us to explore stimulants. I was in the unusual position of having taken them and having had wonderful results. But I was still nervous. The same fears I had for myself resurfaced. I knew in my head that it could help him, but I was scared in my heart. Once again, I had to choose to step forward, when it was frightening to do so.

Parenting an ADHD child

I am fully aware of the weight of this topic. Sometimes I wonder if I should shy away from it because it is so deeply personal and fraught with heavy emotions and feelings. But I am going to be brave and share my experience as a parent of a child with ADHD, who also has ADHD themselves.

As you've read in previous chapters, my son was diagnosed at 6 years old and, at that point, I felt the same way that many other parents feel. I was scared, sad, defiant, angry, devastated and shocked. But there was also a palpable sense of relief. I went through a gamut of emotions, from being made aware that he wasn't the same as most of the other kids, to finally realising that the way he behaved was due to challenges he faced, to embracing his diagnosis and realising that I, too, had the same thing.

Two years on from that and my life looked completely different. My ideas about parenting and what that should look like had been chewed up, spat out and turned to mulch in the garden.

Prior to ADHD becoming apparent in our lives, I had set views on how to parent. I was the boss and that was that. I realise now that I felt so out of control internally that I fought tooth and nail to maintain any sort of control externally.

Unfortunately, my beautiful, gentle first son bore the brunt of that. I overreacted to small things, and I was ready to explode at any moment. Anything that was slightly out of routine threw me. He was such a sweet child, but I still didn't cope well. The thing is though, he was and still is an incredibly resilient kid. So, he went with it and just took it in his stride. Sometimes I cracked the shits at him about something, then went to apologise and it was clear he'd already forgotten about it.

Then my second son came along and didn't just throw the rulebook out of the window – it got flung into a puddle and run over by a truck. Years before his diagnosis, I started to notice that when I shouted at him, he was genuinely shocked. I thought he was being naughty on purpose but, over time, I could see that he honestly didn't know that what he was doing was wrong.

I started to realise that I had to be very specific with my directions with him. It wasn't enough to say, "Don't draw on the walls" because to him that would mean don't draw on the walls of the room we are in, right at that moment. He would forget or not make the connection that I meant every single wall in the whole house. And other people's houses. And doctors' offices. Found that one out the hard way.

I could also see that a disciplinarian style of parenting didn't work for him. Not only was it completely ineffective, but I could also see that it was emotionally hurting him. He would withdraw, and I could tell I was breaking his trust. There was no brushing it off for him. He would take a long time to recover from my outbursts.

> ❝ *I was able to start challenging my ideas about what I thought parenting should look like.* ❞

He dealt with things differently to his big brother. All his emotions lived on the outside of his body, and he was prepared to tell me all about them in the most abrasive and unrepenting way: huge meltdowns, kicking and screaming, breaking things, swearing and hitting, biting and punching his way through life.

To this day I don't quite know how someone like me, who parented by controlling and overpowering her children, somehow saw past that. I truly don't. I was a hard-arsed bitch who was the boss. Nobody messed with me, least of all my kids. But somehow, something within me recognised a glimmer within him. My brain was telling me that he was being naughty, but my heart was screaming that he needed help. I am forever grateful that I listened to my heart. Making that choice has changed our story in the most spectacular way. I was able to start challenging my ideas about what I thought parenting should look like. I could feel myself becoming a bit softer and freeing myself from feeling like I had to have a tight stranglehold over everything. And, in turn, he surprised me by responding positively. I could literally see when my parenting was working.

I started to see that I couldn't simply make a request and know that he would follow through on it. I had to remind him many times, but I knew then that he wasn't misbehaving; he just hadn't heard or didn't remember I had said it. Or, he was far more interested in what he was doing than my request. It was high on my priority list but not his.

At night, if I'd been harsh during the afternoon, he would toss and turn, unable to get to sleep. But when I was gentle, he drifted off with relative ease. I stopped trying to make him put himself to sleep and I sat with him instead. I slowed down and he met me there.

That's not to say that with these realisations I just canned how I had been parenting and revolutionised what I had been doing. Nope. At that time, I was still deep in undiagnosed ADHD myself. I was doing my best to improve but life was a massive jumble, and I didn't have much room to grow. My own problems were still so overwhelming that it was one step forward and seven steps back. I knew something wasn't right, but I didn't know what it was. I was locked in a shame spiral where I wanted to do better, but I couldn't.

I wanted to do better, but I couldn't

This chapter mentions stimulant medication. It is my intention to share my and my family's story as an anecdotal example of our experience. This is not medical advice, and you should always seek the advice of a medical professional for advice, diagnosis and treatment. Never disregard professional medical advice or delay in seeking it because of something you have read in this book.

I wanted to do better, but I <u>couldn't</u>.

I was a grown adult who was educated, emotionally intelligent, well-travelled, a good friend, a hard worker, healthy, fit, kind and generous. But I could not physically and emotionally stop myself from losing my shit and having angry outbursts. I couldn't stop myself from having meltdowns.

Sensory overload would kick in and I lashed out, leaving a path of destruction in my wake. When I had finally sunk down gratefully into the couch at the end of the day, one of my boys would get back up out of bed and disturb me while I was trying to relax. I had spent the day making mistakes and trying to cover them up. I had been in trouble with my boss for not being organised or

I'd forgotten about a meeting I was supposed to go to. All the pressure of the day would be built up like a steam engine and smoke would come billowing out. All my boy wanted was one drink of water, or a cuddle, but to me it was like an insult to my psyche. I had struggled through the whole day and all I wanted to do was lounge on the couch in peace.

Afterwards, I would apologise hollowly, knowing that I wasn't capable of not doing it again. I felt like a hypocrite. And then when they finally slept, I would send myself off to sleep with tears dripping into my ears. I would tell myself that I was a piece of shit. I couldn't believe that these poor kids had to have me as a mother.

My brain couldn't see any positivity past the storm cloud of meltdown. I couldn't see how I had taken the time to make delicious lunches for them, making sure to remember what each child wanted that week. I didn't see how I took the time to play with them or read to them. How I had approached their teacher to discuss how we could make improvements for them in the classroom, or how I made sure they had 734 kisses before they went to sleep.

I didn't see the way they watched me stick up for myself, so they could see how to do that themselves. I didn't see how I remained calm in a scary situation so they could take their cue from me. All that my brain could see was where I had fucked up.

Now, try to imagine that situation but it's your child experiencing it.

Your child has gotten home from a hard day at school. They had to try so hard to concentrate but the other kids were making a lot of noise and your child finds that incredibly distracting. The teacher rushed them in their schoolwork but they didn't understand the directions so they couldn't get it done. Another child laughed at them behind the teacher's back, so your child got angry and yelled at the other kid. But it was only them who got told off.

They got home and sunk down gratefully onto the couch to watch their favourite show, and you asked them to do their homework. All the pressure of the day would be built up like a steam engine and smoke would come billowing out. All you wanted was for them to do their homework but to them it was like an insult to their psyche.

They had struggled through the whole day and all they wanted was some peace. And then, finally, when they went to bed, they would tell themselves that they were a piece of shit. They couldn't believe that you had to have them as a kid.

They couldn't see any positivity past the storm cloud of meltdown. They couldn't see how they helped a friend that day, and how they worked so hard to do what was expected of them. They couldn't remember how even though it was difficult, they ignored a kid who kept teasing them at lunch instead of retaliating. They didn't see how they made you smile so much because they were brave. All their brain could see was where they had fucked up.

Your child wants to do better, but sometimes they *can't*.

You might be thinking that it's different for an adult and a child. Why is that though? Because they're younger? Because we are "the boss"? Are their lives and feelings and emotions any less important than ours as adults? I don't think so.

Of course, there are times where we must be the parent. If it was up to my kids, they would live on lollies and soft drink. They wouldn't have a bedtime or have to do any chores. But it's my job to put those things in place because they need to have healthy food, so their bodies are healthy, to help their brains develop, and so they don't have a million holes in their teeth. They need sleep so that their bodies can rest and recharge. I get them to do chores because I think it teaches life skills and responsibility.

None of these things will impact my children negatively. But when it comes to emotional regulation, they are allowed the grace of not being that great at it. I've given myself that grace, so I extend that to them too.

I have found that since being medicated myself, my ability to be a rational person has increased tenfold. It turns out that I'm not a piece of shit. I just have a neurological disorder that was creating so much chaos and anxiety inside my body that I was completely unable to behave in a way that was acceptable or rational.

My brain was so foggy and overwhelmed that I went straight to meltdown mode in an instant. I was on the edge of losing it at any given moment. But I was pretending that I was okay so that no one else outside of my house would know. Medication eradicated the anxiety and untangled the mess inside of me. It, quite simply, changed my life.

I see many parents in online support groups who are broken, terrified, drained and lost. Parents who are angry or have given up. It is incredibly important to me that what I am writing is in no way from a place of judgement. My heart hurts for those of you who are feeling these things because it's scary and confusing.

But I am going to be honest with you and tell you that my heart hurts more for those children. Having been through this myself, as a fully formed adult, I had the ability to question what was happening to me. I could do my own research, speak to people, write and move through all the emotions. Children don't have that. They can only go by what they are feeling and the external messages they are getting. They already feel like shit, so they don't need reminders that they have yet again not met a societal expectation.

For the first year after his diagnosis, my son was on anti-anxiety medication. He had been showing signs of claustrophobia and extreme anxiety. These feelings exacerbated his ADHD as his little body felt so out of control that he couldn't live his life to the fullest. Even though this was not a stimulant, I was still terrified. I worried that it would change his personality, dull his shine, or somehow make him not himself.

Thankfully, it did none of these things. When he'd been taking the anti-anxiety medication for a few weeks (it takes a while to see the full effect), I asked him if he felt any different. He said, "I'm not scared of doors closing anymore."

For a 6-year-old boy who had not been able to have any door closed while he was in the room, this was a life-changer. Prior to medication, whenever he went into a room, he had to pre-plan his escape. Like the time we went to a public toilet and the main door was a swing-shut one, but it had a lock on the outside that the cleaners would use to lock up at the end of the day.

He was fixated on this lock and how someone could lock it while we were in there. It didn't matter how rational my answers were, he couldn't accept them. Imagine being 6 and having that weight on your shoulders. Heartbreaking. So, to go from that to breezing into the public restroom without a care was wonderful.

After a year of the anti-anxiety medication, I noticed

that it wasn't as effective as it had been. He reported having trouble concentrating in school. His teachers reported the opposite. On the surface he was fantastic, he worked hard and paid attention in class. But it was at a personal cost.

After school he was highly strung and prone to emotional outbursts. By now, I was well versed in masking, which is the act of learning to behave a particular way so that you fit into neurotypical societal expectations. And we all know how well that worked out for me. I wasn't going to take the teachers' word for it – if he said he was struggling, then I wasn't going to make him do it alone. We consulted with his paediatrician, and on his advice started him on a stimulant.

I was in the unique position of having seen the positive effect stimulant medication had on me. I felt grateful that I could try it first and see how beneficial it was. Prior to my own diagnosis and medication, I couldn't wrap my head around how something that is designed to "stimulate" could do the opposite thing and calm an ADHD person down.

I know that medication is a point of contention, stress and worry for a lot of parents. The idea that you will be giving your precious child something like dexamphetamine or methylphenidate hydrochloride is scary! It just is. Even though I had a good response with a stimulant medication myself, I was still concerned that it would affect his personality, disrupt his sleep or change him in some irreversible way.

Despite these reservations, I knew I had to do what was best for him. His paediatrician prescribed dexamphetamine, and should he have a good response to that, he could move to the same medication as me. The results were instant, and after a few days on his new medication he summed it up:

"It feels like there were too many thoughts in my head and now the medication has taken most of them out."

What a relief. I noticed that he was more relaxed and more able to focus too. But he was still the same awesome kid he always had been – he was still loud, quirky and hilarious. He was happy. He still has ADHD, which means he will still have his own unique difficulties. But medication has given him a chance to quell the overwhelming stress messages his body was getting. His brain isn't jumbled like a washing machine anymore. His body isn't uncomfortable and wracked with anxiety. It gives him the freedom to receive information without it being clouded by overwhelming stimuli. I'm so grateful that I could help my son to have a better chance at life.

I'm not pretending to be perfect – my kids have too much screen time, I let them swear, we eat dinner in front of the television and sometimes I make them wear the same dirty school uniform they wore the day before. They fight like WWE wrestlers, I let my older son stay up way too late and when they're acting like a dick, I tell them that they're being a dick.

I still shout sometimes. But instead of it being multiple times a day, it's now maybe once every few days. And it's not to the severity it once was. I can now rationalise before I lose my temper. I am surer of myself. I can catch myself before I get to boiling point, but most of the time I don't get to boiling point at all. I can think clearly and deal with things positively. Most of all I give myself a break. If I have a moment where I'm not proud of how I dealt with something, then I own it and I work on it. And I don't ruminate over it for the rest of the day. I am perfectly flawed and I'm not pretending that I'm anything else.

I can absolutely tell you, hand on heart, that I could not feel the way I feel now without medication. By being kind to myself and getting myself help, I have been able to soften my heart, which has led to so many beautiful things. It has allowed me to give my son the grace to be perfectly imperfect, just like me. And from that, he has been able to flourish.

I can't (and wouldn't) tell you what to do with your child. But I hope that by sharing my story, it may allow you to see things from your child's perspective a little more. And it might help to forge success in one of the most important relationships you will ever have in your life.

Just in case you wonder how I measure my success, it's when I receive birthday cards like this. The year my son turned 7, and shortly after starting his medication. To be clear, we *all* thought it was funny, even his brother. And I did warn you that I let my kids swear.

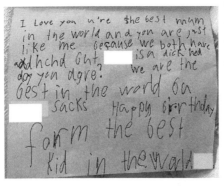

"I love you, you're the best mum in the world and you are just like me because we both have ADHD but *'brother'* is a dickhead, do you agree? We are the best in the world but *'brother'* sucks. Happy birthday from the best kid in the world."

It even rhymes. I don't think there is anything much better than that.

Connection with your child

If you asked me what the single most important thing is in helping someone to manage their symptoms, I would quickly answer medication. But a close second to that would have to be connection.

As I've mentioned, my son was diagnosed when he was in Year 1 at school after his teacher, who also has a son with ADHD, brought her concerns to me. Her son is an adult now, but she obviously remembered her son when he was the same age as mine. Being faced with a diagnosis is daunting, particularly one that is so badly represented and misunderstood. His teacher never shamed him for his ADHD behaviour. Now that's not to say that she just let him get away with anything. Not in the slightest. In fact, he missed out on the end-of-term celebration because he had behaved negatively in her classroom.

The thing is though, she adored my son. And he knew she loved him. Not a surface love. This woman genuinely gave a shit about my son. And *he could tell*. That's the important bit. He knew that even if he was being given boundaries and then having things taken away because he had stepped over those boundaries, he knew she was on his side. I'm not talking about unreasonable boundaries like expecting him to sit still, or being made to work as fast as the other children. I'm referring to things like not being rude to her or the other children. Or no swearing. She made accommodations for things he could not help and boundaries for those he could.

As a result, he felt safe. He knew what the limits were. She encouraged him to go and run on the oval when she saw him jiggling in his seat. He was able to bring in a big beanbag and fling himself onto it when he needed to move. He was granted permission to chew gum in class because she noticed he would chew on his clothing and that one of his sensory input needs was oral.

> ❝ *If I get so much as a sniff of judgement, then there I will be – advocating for my son.* ❞

When he missed out on the end-of-term celebration my heart ached. I wanted to fight against it and argue with her. Instead, I made the monumental decision to step back and let her do what she was clearly put on this earth to do. And guess what? The world didn't stop turning. And the next term when he returned, I could see a difference. She had laid down a healthy boundary, while still accommodating his needs, and I could see him unfurling like a sapling towards the sun.

This teacher set the tone for what I will accept in his schooling life. Thankfully, we live in a small town, and our tiny school has an incredible knack for employing people who think outside the box. The following year he was lucky enough to get another teacher who was on the same level. He knew straight away that she was on his side, and, as a result, he wanted to do his best. As we move through future schooling years, I refuse to budge on the quality of his teachers. If I get so much as a sniff of judgement, then there I will be – advocating for my son.

I see many stories from parents who are having issues with their child and their schooling. And I truly believe, from the bottom of my heart, that what is missing is connection. The thing about kids with ADHD is that they have a strong bullshit-o-meter. They have a super-fast processor in their brains so they can see through the fluff, and they *know* when someone is genuinely on their side. Being on their side doesn't mean they just get away with everything. It means they have a safe place where they are given appropriate accommodations with kind, firm and reliable limits.

Children with ADHD who are struggling are asking for your help. They don't know why they feel the way they do. Hell, I was a well-educated woman with great self-reflection skills, and I still didn't know why I felt the way I did! Children can't articulate what is wrong, so they ask for help in the most negative way possible. Their way of being happy may not look the way you think it should. You might stress that they are on their screens too much. But what if that screen is their source of helping their body to make dopamine? If someone told me over and over that the one thing that was making me feel better was in fact wrong, and that I should feel ashamed about it, then I would feel crappy too.

It's time for us to shed the ideas around parenting that are totalitarian. Given the chance, your children will show you what they need to thrive. Being their champion and steadfastly on their side is something you will never regret. Show up for them. Advocate for them. Challenge what you have been doing if it's not working and do something different.

I asked my son when he was 7½ years old what the main thing was that had helped him with ADHD. I was expecting him to say his medication, but without missing a beat, this kid – who is rarely serious – looked me dead in the eye and said, "You."

Excuse me, I appear to have something in my eye.

Me? The imperfect idiot who makes mistakes all the time? Who can't get to appointments early? Who forgets people's birthdays and says inappropriate things? Who yells and swears and has to apologise all the time? The one who was so mean to herself that she felt worthless? Me? I was the person who helped my son the most with his ADHD. That's got to be my greatest achievement to date.

Support groups

That connection for your child is just as important for you too. After all, we all have an inner child that is crying out for connection. Don't roll your eyes – we do! Especially if you are an adult who until recently didn't know that you had ADHD. Or you are an adult who knew they had ADHD, but your emotional needs were not being met.

Connection doesn't always have to be between two people. It can be a connection with yourself. Pre-diagnosis, when I first had my suspicions about ADHD, I started being kinder to myself. Now that I had a possible reason for why I was the way I was, I could give myself a goddam break.

One of the greatest things I've done on my ADHD journey of self-discovery is to join online ADHD groups. I highly recommend this. I found my groups on Facebook – I purposely searched for groups for women and joined a worldwide one and an Australian one.

Now, my past experiences with groups on Facebook has been somewhat chequered. There seems to be a certain type of person in online groups, doesn't there? There is always the one who is a dickhead, the one who gets into fights, the one who doesn't get it, the one who posts way too many times a day – and then all the "normal" people who you never seem to hear from because they're drowned out by the above.

Do yourself a favour and join a group in the neuro-diverse community. You have never been amongst more loving, caring and helpful people in your life. For the first time, I felt seen, heard and, most importantly, understood. The comparison between this and a local community group, which I was kicked out of because I complained when the admin was repeatedly sexist and racist, was monumental. In ND groups I am me, and they are them, and we are also all part of something bigger. There is no judgement, only love.

One of the main things I struggled with before my diagnosis was asking for help. I spent my whole life pretending I was on top of things, so I didn't want people to think I was failing because I asked for help. Pretty hefty stuff, right? That's a lot to carry on your shoulders, no matter how strong you are. It's also quite arrogant when I think about it. *I didn't like being told what to do, so I immediately discounted asking for advice in case I had to take it.*

The first time I asked for help was in a Facebook group. My son was 7 at the time and was struggling with self-esteem. I was at a complete loss as to how to react. I had tried various things in the past, but I still felt ill-equipped to help him.

I did something I had never done before, and I asked for suggestions in an ADHD parenting group. Within half an hour I had 10 solid, helpful suggestions. Ones that aligned with my parenting style, ones that taught me something, and ones that other people commented on because they'd helped them too.

Who would have thought? Asking for help wasn't admitting a weakness. It was saying, "Hey, I don't know it all, any ideas?" It was drawing on other people's experiences and learning from them. It was drawing on love and compassion and allowing myself the grace of saying I was struggling.

I didn't feel weak. I felt supported and seen. I felt the collective love of people who had been there themselves and who took the time to share what had helped them. I wasn't being strong by denying myself that assistance. I was being strong by admitting that I didn't know it all.

Talks too much!

People in your life

I see a recurring theme from fellow ADHD folk who are criticised by the people around them. Either these people doubt the diagnosis, they discourage you from seeking one, they make nasty comments, or they blame you for things that are not your fault. I am here to tell you that it is possible to only have people around you who support you.

For people with ADHD, it's especially paramount that we have people around us who love and support us as we are. We spend our lives getting messages that our behaviour isn't acceptable, so having a safe place to land is imperative.

I know you can't avoid crappy people your whole life – we have all had that arsehole co-worker – but the people you *choose* (and, yes, I am including family in that) can be supportive and loving. And I don't mean they just bow down before you and kiss your feet. I mean, I wouldn't say no but... no, that's weird.

Quality people will support you when you need it, give you feedback when you need it and pull you up if you start being a douche. Which is why I am down to 3 friends. I'm kidding. (Am I?) No, seriously. I do this unofficial categorisation of people I know.

Category one: The golden people

These are the ride-or-dies, the no-matter-whats. The ones you feel always surround you with a golden ball of light and you feel warm and fuzzy when you spend time with them. BUT... and this is the kicker... you don't *have* to spend time with them to maintain that. You can go for months, hell you can go for years without even speaking a word to them. You might maintain that golden cord between you by liking each other's Instagram snaps. You might watch all their stories. The friendship just is.

But you also know that if you saw them on the street, you would gasp and *run towards them.* I need to emphasise this. You would voluntarily move towards them, greet them and have a conversation.

When I was doing the guest list for my wedding, I based it on people who fell into this category. If I didn't gasp when I saw them (and I don't mean in a "Shit, where can I hide" way), then they didn't make the cut. These people were the ones I knew I could talk to about my suspicions about having ADHD. This is *very* different to telling people I've been diagnosed with ADHD. Very, very different. To be able to trust people with a hunch you have about yourself and know that they won't say, "YOU?! Don't be stupid! Oh, go on... we ALLLL have ADHD!" is a special thing.

So, we have established that you may not see these people all the time. But when you do see them, you just pick up where you left off. There is never any weirdness. And you know everything that has been going on in their life because you watch their stories, right? Or you know nothing, and you get to have one of those long, delicious and juicy catchups where you overshare everything. These are the people who give you full, hard, lengthy hugs. Real pelvis to pelvis action. These are good people.

I remember taking my eldest son to the park with friends when he was a baby. I would just rock up with him. Nothing else. My best friend had twins and she would arrive with a nappy bag, nappies, spare clothes, drink bottles, wipes and a change mat. As well as – and this was the kicker – prepared food. Like cut up, ready-to-eat food. It didn't matter how many times we went to the park; it was always the same.

Meanwhile, I was *always* surprised when my son needed a nappy change or a change of clothes. Even though he needed those things multiple times a day, I did not remember that. Luckily for me, my best friend just accepted that was how I was and offered me a spare nappy, or just packed more food. How good is that? Someone meeting you halfway and just accepting how you are – and making accommodations to allow for you.

Category two: The distance people

These are the people I really quite like but also keep a bit of a distance from. This is a broad category. It can range from a relative whom you feel fond of, but you're not speaking to regularly, and you don't receive any emotional support from. It's also your boss, your kids' coach...

You would stop to talk to them if you saw them in the street but, and this is important, *you wouldn't gasp*. Funnily enough, you can still confide in these people. Sometimes the distance allows a freedom you might not find in other relationships. They're more like a once-in-a-blue-moon interaction, but that doesn't mean they can't give you a lovely connection.

These people can also be strangers, and the interaction can be fleeting and a once-off. Or they can be people you work with, mums of your friends' kids or the local barista. You can share with these people.

I can think of so many different little conversations I've had where I openly shared what was going on with me and the other person reciprocated. Personally, I think oversharing is a great thing – it allows others to feel as though they can share with you. It breaks down this weird barrier people have up where they want to hide their problems, or they feel ashamed.

Sometimes these people turn into the golden people. Sometimes they just stay the slightly distanced people. But either way, they're one of the good guys.

Category three: The dicks

I can barely even be bothered to write about these idiots. These are the people who say, "EVErYonE has ADHD", or, "You're just using that as an excuse", or, "People like you are just after the medication". Personally, I haven't come across too many of these people because I've carefully surrounded myself with not-dicks. If I meet a dick, they don't make it past the first dick-ish show of behaviour and I de-dick them out of my life. Man, that's a lot of dicks.

You may have a dick in your life. Not a sentence I thought I was going to write, but there we are.

The thing is, you don't have to keep dicks around. You can put up boundaries, you can remove them from your social media, and you can hide behind a mannequin when you see them at the shops. It sounds simple, doesn't it? That's because it is. One of the places you're most likely to run into dicks is on the internet. It seems to be a breeding ground for them. Don't make the mistake of trying to argue with them in the comments section, just delete and block. Trust me.

One of the biggest parts of my journey so far has been learning the ability to set up boundaries. About a year before I even suspected I had ADHD I started putting up boundaries. I was working part-time but was being treated like I worked full-time with the number of work-related calls I got on my day off. I was really struggling personally at the time and had attempted to put up a boundary by reducing my days at work. Turns out that this only works if people then do the crucial part of *leaving you alone on your day off*.

The problem is that some people still won't listen, even when you make a specific request. It's up to you to decide how you deal with that. I left the job. I don't think that's too dramatic either. I was being shown that my boundaries did not matter to them. They didn't respect my wishes, and I knew I had a choice. I could stick it out and suck it up, and slowly become more and more miserable, or I could respect myself enough to walk away. I think we get so caught up in a situation that we can't see what is on the other side.

You may have spent your whole life either feeling like there is something wrong with you, being told there is something wrong with you, or being given subliminal messages that there is something wrong with you. After a while, it's hard not to take on the same view.

As a result, you may not value yourself enough to think you are worthy of being surrounded by the golden people and having the distance people on the periphery. I can assure you that you most definitely are. There isn't something "wrong" with you – you are a unique person who deals with things in a different way to a large part of the population. It's not wrong. It's *different*. And anyone who tries to make you feel any other way is the one who is wrong.

It's bloody hard to deal with when these people are your family or your romantic partner. From my observations, it is common for women, particularly those with ADHD and other co-morbid conditions, to accept behaviour from those close to them that is unacceptable.

It is not okay for people to make you feel as though you are "less than". It is not okay for people to dismiss your diagnosis or say mean things to you. We also have the added pressure of suffering from things such as rejection sensitive dysphoria or impostor syndrome, which means we often don't trust our own opinions and ideas.

I know that when I get into a disagreement I am easily bamboozled by the other person. Particularly when they are a manipulative narcissist. Please don't waste your life being around people who make you feel anything other than great about who you are. That's not to say you won't have disagreements and misunderstandings because you will. But you will also have love and forgiveness and communication.

There are a LOT of good people out there. There really are. Sometimes you are so clouded by the dicks that you can't see the golden ones. But they are there. Keep an eye out. You might have to be brave and step out of your comfort zone to speak to them first, but it will be worth it. Don't be discouraged if you get it wrong every now and then. After a time, you will learn to spot the signs of the good ones.

Being a woman with ADHD

Social conditioning has a lot to answer for. When I was growing up in the *cough* '80s and '90s *cough*, girls were supposed to be quiet and behave. It wasn't "normal" for a girl to speak up and have opinions. Most certainly not strong ones that they said out loud.

Something my ex said to me early on in our relationship remains one of the most defining moments of my life. I can remember exactly where I was when he said it. I can recall exactly how it felt. We were discussing something, and he interrupted me with, "Do you have to be SO opinionated?"

Well, shit, I thought, *You just said that like it was a bad thing.*

I was in my early 20s. He was 10 years older. I thought the sun and moon shone clear out of his butt and, as soon as he said it, I felt myself shrink. There was the message that being loud and, perish the thought, having an opinion, was BAD. Capital letters B-A-D.

This had not been my first experience with this opinion. I had spent my whole life being told I was too much, too loud, too good at sport, too smart, too proud of myself.

I was told this by boys while I was at school. And by men, as I became a woman. I had too much to say and I wasn't scared to say it. I was being force-fed the message that I shouldn't be myself. I didn't understand how you could be anything except yourself. What were you if you weren't yourself?

In high school, I watched the popular girls giggle and flick their hair, laughing at the boys' (crappy) jokes. I could not do that. They weren't funny! Gradually, I began to see that if you want people to like you, you laugh at boys' crappy jokes, otherwise you are a bitch. You keep your opinions to yourself unless they're the same opinions as everyone else's. And you most certainly don't speak up when you see something happening that's wrong.

Boys were bewildered by me. I was great at sport, smart as a whip, funny, loud, had great banter and told it how it was. So, naturally, teenage boys found that threatening, and I was teased and called a boy. They took my amazing qualities and tried to appoint them as male traits. Typical.

But still, as a child and young woman, I persevered at this funny notion of being myself. A push against societal expectations. I wanted to be heard and I didn't care what other people thought. I had an amazing family who embraced this and a group of awesome friends who loved me as I was.

For some reason though, when I was in my early 20s, hearing that sentence come out of my then boyfriend's mouth, something in me shrank. At that moment I made the mistake that so many women make. I began to try to make myself fit into someone else's ideals. I was being criticised, and instead of pushing back and standing my ground, I folded and felt ashamed. Maybe I *was* too opinionated. Maybe I should tone it down a bit. If I wanted him to stick around, then that looked like the natural conclusion to me.

Too often, a woman's answer to being criticised or questioned is to conform.

Our answer to being told that our behaviour is wrong is to believe it and try to change ourselves.

Never mind that it's cranky old Aunt Mary who said it, and she says that to everyone. Or your super-critical friend who seems to have a problem with anyone who isn't her. For whatever reason, you are essentially being told that YOU are WRONG.

When you're told by someone externally that you are wrong, maybe you can brush it off. But if you're being told that you're wrong over and over, then you start to internalise it. And you notice that other people seem to be able to deal with things better than you. You don't understand why inside of you feels so uncomfortable, and you just assume that there is simply just something wrong with you.

Traditionally, women are underdiagnosed with ADHD because it can present in such a different way to how young boys exhibit it. My hyperactivity is all internal. I can say with complete confidence that if you had asked anyone I knew well if I had ADHD, they wouldn't have let you finish before they were confidently saying no.

Such was my shame about my lack of coping skills, I didn't externalise any of my problems. I adopted the more socially acceptable explanation of anxiety. What I didn't express were my suspicions that there was something else wrong too. But I was so ashamed that I just decided I would put up with it and assume that was the way it was going to be forever. Clearly, I was a failure, but it was my fault, so I didn't deserve to ask for help.

Let's talk about how ADHD may look in women. And let's be clear, you *do not* have to have all these symptoms. ADHD looks different in everyone:

- Feeling overwhelmed by busy places – shops, the office or at social gatherings.
- Not being able to ignore sounds and distractions.
- Feeling like you never have enough time, like money is always an issue, like you're surrounded by paperwork, or "stuff".
- Getting to the point where you just shut down. Day or night, you get to the point where you feel "under attack" from the demands placed on you. And someone asking for that one last thing tips you over the emotional edge.
- Do you feel like your days are just filled with you simply coping? Always looking for things? Always catching up, or having to cover up? Avoiding other people because you're so overwhelmed? For example, you just had those papers you needed for your boss, but now they've disappeared. You lie and say you'll get them to your boss as soon as you can, not knowing how you will find them again.
- Have you been avoiding inviting people over because you can't stay on top of the mess in your house? Or you do the frantic tidy up just before they arrive to "act normal" so they won't find out what is really going on.
- What about problems with staying on top of your finances? Overspending and then feeling guilty?

You may have a lack of impulse control when it comes to buying things. I mean, I'm not gonna judge you for the pet llama you have in your backyard, but you would know it wasn't the best idea to buy him when you have outstanding bills to pay.

- Life may constantly feel out of control. You may feel like there is no way of ever meeting all the demands put on you.
- Feeling like it's all or nothing. You are either stuck to the couch with no motivation, or you're running around like a cyclone.
- Sometimes you have it all together and everything is working well, then with no warning the wheels fall off and it's all back to being a shitshow.
- You may have amazing ideas, but you don't feel capable of organising them or carrying them out.
- You may start each day convinced that this is the day you will be on top of things, only to end the day feeling overwhelmed and beaten down.
- Do you feel like other people who have the same level of education as you, or an equal level of intelligence, seem to fly past you with achievements?
- Do you worry that you may never meet your goals or reach your potential?
- How about wondering why you just can't seem to manage small tasks, like sending a birthday card? Knowing the date is bearing down on you but, for some reason, you just can't manage it?
- Do you look at other people and wonder how they seem to be able to live their life in a way that seems consistent? I often wonder how other

people appear to just take things in their stride and not get bogged down in the "stuff" of life?

- Are you called a "slob" or "spacey"? Are you "passing for normal"? Do you feel as if you are an impostor?
- Is all your time and energy taken up with coping, staying organised and holding it together, with no time for fun or relaxation?
- Do you find that time gets away from you and you have no idea where it went?

It's important to note that you probably have *some, not all*, of these symptoms. That doesn't mean you don't have ADHD. Each person's experiences are different based on so many other factors – life experiences, genetic makeup, family dynamics and personality.

I felt on edge *all the time*. I mean, I had heard about relaxation, of course, but to me it felt like looking at someone's social media – it sounds and looks good, but is it real? I couldn't imagine being in a situation where my body would relax enough that I could then feel calm. My body physically always felt tense. I held my stomach tightly, my jaw was rock-solid, and I felt like I had a heavy weight sitting on my chest. Not for one single second did I imagine those feelings were coming from ADHD. Never in a million years. I self-diagnosed with chronic anxiety and just tried to accept that was how it was.

I tried meditating, particularly during and after my breakdown. But guess what meditation did? It made me so anxious to have to sit still and close my eyes that I spent the whole time trying not to have a panic attack. I had to peek my eyes open to stop from losing my shit.

Such was my disregard for honouring myself, I persisted in trying to do something that wasn't helping just because other people said it helped them. Then I would feel bad because I wasn't trying hard enough to help myself. I kept waiting for that one time when I'd start meditating and I would finally stick at it and be fixed.

I was waiting for the time that I'd learn to breathe right, and then I'd be fixed. I was living inside a hurricane and trying to hold on to a piece of floss for stability. I would have a massage to "relax" and would struggle to not have a panic attack when I closed my eyes. I would visit the dentist and have to fight the urge to jump out of the chair and kick over the trolley while escaping, clattering dental tools all over the place.

When I look back, I can see that my body did not respond well to being – for want of a better word – trapped. I felt like I was being held hostage because these were situations where it was not socially acceptable to be continually moving in the way I needed to, to combat these feelings.

The things that were supposed to make me feel better (dentist notwithstanding), according to the world, were not working.

Talks too much!

ADHD and the mental load

The mental load can go and suck a big one – *amiright?* Why do women carry most of the mental load of our families? Yes, I AM AWARE that *some* men take on some of the mental load. THAT IS WONDERFUL. However, this is a book for women with ADHD (or people wanting to support women with ADHD), and, as a result, I will be focusing on that perspective. Because in the MAJORITY of families, the women shoulder these things. Jeez, that was a lot of CAPITAL letters there.

And as women we get told that we are supposed to be able to manage it all. Here is an annoyingly long list of all the shit I have to think about in an average week:

- Organising birthday presents for friends and family – remembering dates and figuring out what the person likes. The WORST is when I have to post a gift by a certain time.
- Posting letters – having an envelope and then finding a stamp, and then remembering to put it in my car to post the stupid thing. Then driving past the mailbox without stopping for the next two weeks.

- Signing and returning forms to school – making sure I get them out of the kids' bags (because why the hell would my kids remember to hand me them?), then filling them out and trying to get them back to school by the due date.
- Organising doctors' appointments – not just for myself, but for my kids. Being aware of which doctor is for which thing and keeping track of the appointments once they're made. This is particularly painful when it comes to an appointment that is not straightforward, like trying to get into a paediatrician.
- Monitoring how my children are feeling – not what they say they're feeling but watching them and reading their emotions and knowing when to leave them alone or when to encourage them to talk.
- Keeping track of referrals. Why is this not online? I can't remember to take my sunglasses; do you think I can take care of those stupid bits of paper?
- Buying shoes – by monitoring the state of the kids' shoes, or when they've grown out of them. Also knowing which type of shoes and socks they need, taking into account sensory issues.
- Organising haircuts.
- Buying groceries. Figuring out meals is an offshoot of this. Shoot me is how I feel about it. Remembering brands that my family likes, what food each person is into. Trying to remember what I have in the fridge.
- Buying medication, keeping track of scripts and making sure my kids and I take their medication.

Including supplements because we must remember to treat the whole person too!

- Making sure everyone is drinking enough water. Sounds simple. It isn't. I have an app that reminds me to drink water. I ignore it almost every time.
- Monitoring screen time. Teetering between the relief of having the kids out of my hair and simultaneously worrying they're going to be serial killers because they've spent 47 hours playing *Fortnite*. Worrying about my own screen time.
- Helping with homework. This is a special kind of hell. Just so you know, "Let's google it" and, "Get the calculator" are valid options.
- Making sure my children's mental health is taken care of. Making sure my own mental health is taken care of.
- Preparing lunches. Hate this. Having enough coordination to have the right food, in date, in the fridge and cupboard ready to go is almost insurmountable.
- Paying the bills. Knowing which bill is due when and for whom and what other bills are coming.
- Being patient and always loving. Because we are women and this is what we MUST do, and if we don't do that, we are failures (insert sarcasm here).

A woman with ADHD trying to shoulder these things is like trying to transport sand in a sieve. It's fucking horrific. We don't naturally have the coping skills to juggle all these things, which we then reflect onto ourselves as not being good enough. And we then try to deal with these things by creating a false self that mimics a neurotypical person. Sounds like a recipe for disaster, doesn't it? I can manage all those things. But to do so I must sacrifice my own happiness, fulfilment, enjoyment and peace of mind. The cost is too high.

I had spent my life being successful. I had a high opinion of myself, and I was critical of myself. Bit of an oxymoron there, hey? I thought I *should be able to* do all these things. And, yes, sometimes I could. But when I couldn't, I was so incredibly mean to myself. I was successful! How come it felt like my life was falling apart all the time?

As my children got older and the responsibility increased, I felt myself spiralling. There would be times where I was killing it, having it all under control. And then, suddenly, the rollercoaster was still going but I had fallen off. Having to be organised for myself was too much. Having to be organised for myself and two kids was impossible. So not only was I regularly dropping the ball, but I was also being mean to myself about it at the same time. I was shrouded in shame.

I lay in bed most nights sobbing over things I'd said and done the day before. My body was so tightly wound that I didn't even know what was normal anymore. I waded through my days trying so hard to manage every little piece of responsibility.

As I mentioned earlier, at one stage I found myself as a single parent. My relationship had broken down. We'd had quite a few good years, but a large part of why we had those good years was because I had successfully moulded myself into who he wanted me to be.

I let so many things go that I didn't agree with because I didn't want to lose him. I had received messages my whole life that I wasn't lovable as myself, and, as a result, there was something deep inside of me that said I'd better hold on to the one guy who would "put up" with me. Albeit a diluted version of myself.

I'd got caught up in the flurry of having a first child, and the subsequent years, then an infertility struggle for my second son, which ended with him being conceived by IVF. After the newborn craziness had worn off, I looked at my ex-partner and knew deeply that not only did he not like me, but I also didn't like him. I use the word "like" intentionally because I think liking someone is in some ways more important than loving them.

I was sick of pretending to be someone I wasn't. I was tired of pretending I had it all together. So, I blew my life apart. I walked away, and it was the best thing I ever did. It was the best thing for both of us, and I believe it was the best thing for the children. It was imperative to me that our children did not grow up seeing their parents fighting all the time. It was so important to me that my boys did not see me in a relationship that was not honouring me. I didn't want them to be adults and emulate what they were seeing.

The great thing is that now we've been apart for some time, we co-parent well. He's supportive of me seeking help for the children and myself and allows me to drive most of the decisions. He's a great father to the boys and we communicate well. We weren't meant to be together forever, but we did manage to make some awesome kids.

Talks too much!

Task fatigue

Hand in hand with the mental load is task fatigue. And decision fatigue. And 'manage to hold my shit together' fatigue.

I'm going to tell you a little story that may resonate with you.

It starts with a simple request from my boys' softball team. We hit the jackpot this one particular year and they both ended up in the same team despite the 5-year age difference. The coach dropped out, so I stepped up to coach.

Each child in the team has to pay cash for umpire fees.

Cash. CASH.

I never, ever, ever have cash. Who does these days, apart from drug dealers and tradies doing cashies on the weekends?

And so begins what I like to refer to as "The Dance of Not Getting Something Seemingly Simple Done". It's *easy*, right? Just get the cash out and pay the money. No.

It's not a task that sits at the forefront of my mind because I have ADHD, and, subsequently, if things are not in front of me, then they don't exist. Also, I have a mental stumbling block over the amount. It's $35 and you can't take that exact amount out of the ATM.

After weeks of forgetting, I finally aligned the gods enough that I left early on the way to a game. I planned my route to go past a petrol station that had an ATM. Task stacking – absolutely love this shit. I am a legend. I can achieve anything.

I got there. I didn't have my card.

The card that NEVER left my purse was not there. Well, it probably was in the purse, but the purse itself was the problem because it appeared to be missing from my car. And the best bit was that I'd seen it that morning, thought, *Nah, I won't need that*, and *left it on the couch.* My kids are used to this kind of malarky by now and don't bat an eyelid.

The following week I was prepared.

By prepared, I mean that I set an alarm to remember to put my purse in the car. I set an alarm to leave early. I set an alarm to go off about the time I would drive past the petrol station. Success! I had my card AND I stopped at the ATM. I got the money out but needed to break one of the $20 notes. Oooh! They had my favourite type of chewing gum. I handed over a note and realised, as I was walking back to the car, that I'd spent too much, and I now didn't have the right amount. Then I had to give my son some cash for the movies.

Now I was short by $20. And because I didn't have the full amount, I didn't hand any of the money over when we got to softball.

Time bowled on and, weeks later, I still hadn't paid the fee.

Welcome to how ADHD likes to kick my arse, my friends. Welcome.

I am the person who must do all the things. And I am also the person who struggles with the things the most. To be perfectly honest with you, I am fucking sick of the tasks. Why are there so many? Surely, this is a universal thing, or are there people out there doing the tasks and doing them well? If so, please send me over some of your DNA so I can drink it. That sounds gross but this is where we are right now.

Task fatigue is just being so overwhelmed with all the things that you want to throw your hands up in the air and move to an ashram in another country. But they'd probably still make me do tasks there too. I'd probably oversee remembering to put the candles out, and we all know how that would go.

Task fatigue can feel a lot like burnout. It can also be referred to as cognitive fatigue. Prior to my realisation that I had ADHD, I thought that what I was feeling was "just" burnout. But to have the combination of undiagnosed ADHD and burnout was the reason I ended up having a breakdown. My body gave up on trying to give me subtle warning signs and instead shut me down so that I had no choice but to pay attention.

The tips and tricks of managing task fatigue, which you commonly read, are ones that are designed by neurotypical people. I can't just decide that I'm going to do something and do it. I need to design an elaborate system of intricate reminders, alarms and carrier pigeons to initiate the chain of events that *might* get me to do a task. I need tips that are designed for my ADHD brain.

Talks too much!

Kind of crap ADHD-friendly hacks

Here is a secret no one tells you: the rules are made up – by neurotypical people who live in a neurotypical world. Their brains work by having a task and then just doing it because they should.

People with ADHD don't work like that. We can feel easily overwhelmed, and then things feel insurmountable. Even setting reminders isn't failsafe because we become desensitised to them and literally can't see them.

But guess what? You don't *have* to do things the way you've always been told to. You can do things in different ways that suit you. You can break those rules altogether. If I'm going to be left with the responsibility of carrying out these annoying chores, then they're getting done my way. Terribly.

Sometimes, it feels like I'm stuck in an ADHD box that I need a staircase to get out of, but I've only been left with the tools to make a ladder. No one told me the ladder would also get me out! And I'm left feeling frustrated because I can't figure out how to build the damn staircase.

Well, guess what? I'm here to tell you that the ladder can get you out just the same as that stupid staircase.

Similarly, these hacks are other ways around that work for me:

- **Task stacking**. You have a few tasks to do that are annoying, but when you put them together, you can ease the annoyance. For example, at one of my jobs the drink fountain and toilet were in the same vicinity as each other. I find it annoying to have to go to the toilet at all, and I also find it taxing to remember to fill my water bottle. But doing them together was so pleasing. Not together … oh, you know what I mean. Add in smuggling my phone into my pocket so I could have a cheeky scroll on Instagram while on the loo. Oh, don't pretend you don't do it too!

- **Wear a work uniform**. No really. I found these pants at Kmart that were only $18. They're black, high-waisted with an elastic waist (forgiving) with pockets. I bought a few pairs and announced that they were now my self-imposed work uniform. I can change the top around, but the pants stay the same. And that has now removed the task of "picking something to wear" every day.

- **Lunch orders**. Hate is too weak a word to use for my feelings about having to make lunches every day. The day they introduced online lunch orders for school was the day the heavens shone upon my addled head. They are the cat's meow. My older son can visit the canteen every day if he needs to. When I can't be bothered, I scrounge up some coins from the floor of my car and off he goes. One less thing to think about. He eats well for breakfast and dinner, so he can eat what he wants for lunch at school.

- **Simplify your banking**. I have a separate bank account purely for bills. It's not a bank account I look at and ALL my bills come from it. I don't want to have to pay a bill physically again until the end of time. It turns out that not all bills can be automated, but I have also worked out how much I need to put aside for all of them and that money goes into that account too. Then when I need to pay it, I just pay it. I used to have this block about paying bills because my fun money and bills money were together. It felt like I was wasting fun money by paying the bills. Now they're separate, so I can have plain old fun with my fun money.

- **Automate all the things**. There are lots of services that will automate things for you. My contact lenses are automated. I can't begin to tell you how much time and energy I wasted trying to get to the store to order them. Now they just come every month, and, to make it even better, it's cheaper to subscribe. I've also automated my laundry liquid and makeup remover – two things that I always run out of and never remember to buy.

- **Store things in the fridge where you can see them**. Who said that we HAVE to keep fruit and vegetables in the fruit and veggie drawer? Instead of letting the poor things languish away, I got some clear containers, I store the veggies in them and have them on a shelf in eyesight. Most ADHD people won't remember something exists if they can't see it. The exception to that rule is the stuff that you won't forget – you know what I'm talking about – the chocolate, the nice drinks.

They can go in the crisper because ain't nobody forgetting about them. And, if you do, then that's okay – they take far longer to go off, and when you find them you have a nice surprise, not a sweating pile of rotten zucchini glue.

- **Click and collect food shopping**. If you don't have this, then I am truly sorry. It has revolutionised my food shopping experience. Trying to coordinate myself to go food shopping was the bane of my existence. I would write a list and always leave it at home. And when was I going to the super-market anyway? Not on the damn weekend when everyone else was there. Yuck. And don't even get me started on taking the kids to the shops. Shopping in person is for suckers. Unless you do it, then it's fine.

   I do mine online. I select the pickup window that coincides with the time I would have been driving past from work anyway. Someone does the shop-ping for me, and I just pick it up. GENIUS! And another little hack is that you can write notes on the items, so if you don't want crappy avocados (pet hate of mine) then you can write annoyingly specific requests like, *Please don't give me really hard or really soft avocados. Just slightly soft.* Not that I know anyone who would write something that irritating. Nuh-uh.

- **Just give up on family meals**. I'm sorry but I am DONE with family meals where we all sit down at the same time. Every once in a while the planets align, and it works that we all eat together. But I am not doing that every night. Instead, we sit on the couch and we watch TV. Judge me if you will. It works and I don't care.

- **Have a crap menu**. It took me a long time to realise that if I was going to be held responsible for the family menu, then I could do what I wanted. And what I wanted was to make the same thing over and over and over. About 90 percent of the meals I prepare for the kids are plates of chopped-up fruit and veg, with some sort of protein cooked in the air fryer. Sometimes I mix it up but (and this is the important bit) *only if I can be bothered*. If someone in my family wants something different, then they can feel free to do it themselves.

- **Get an air fryer**. Seriously, just do it. I cook everything in there in a fraction of the time. It's a no-brainer and I won't hear a bad word against them. Get the oven-style one with the drawers so you can cook multiple things at a time. Mine is also a dehydrator. Have I ever used it for that? No. I felt like that might sway you though, if you like that sort of thing.

- **You don't have to make a meal to eat it**. Okay, so hear me out. You might feel like a salad but it's too overwhelming to make one. Just eat the parts of a salad. Just grab a handful of lettuce or spinach or rocket and eat that. Then eat some tomato. Eat some cucumber. Have a handful of grated cheese. Eat a tin of tuna or some roast chicken (pre-made, nobody is making that themselves) and presto! You have eaten a salad. You're welcome.

- **Brush your teeth whenever you remember**. Now, I love brushing my teeth for some reason, so I don't struggle to remember this. But I do task stack and do it in the shower. While reading a book. *Shhh*, I have ADHD. But if you struggle to remember and then you remember at lunchtime, just do it then. Brushing at any time is better than never. But even if you never do it, I see you and I love you and you are perfect in my eyes.

- **Phone chargers**. Guess what? You can have *as many of these as you like.* You can. And they're cheap. You can get them for about $15. Have them in every room, in your car, in your office ... anywhere you want to charge your phone. It took me a mortifyingly long time to come to this realisation.

- **Just do 15 minutes of exercise**. Exercise is a bone of contention for me. If I didn't have two big dogs, I doubt I would go for a walk. But I also know that I like doing weights. But liking doing them and doing them are two different things. So now, I wake up and before I can think about it, I go down to my shed in my pyjamas and I do 15 minutes of weights. Sometimes, I don't even put a bra on!

  Yes, I could take out an eye but if I had to put a bra on then the motivation would be gone. I can never find a sports bra and I'm not about to start managing to remember to prepare one the night before. So off I go, tits akimbo, and do my 15 minutes while listening to a podcast or music to keep me engaged. Am I going to be the next top model? No. Was I ever going to be? Also no.

But is 15 minutes of exercise better than none? Absolutely.

- **Voice notes**. Introduce the absolute joy that is voice notes to your friends. If you're like me, then you find it hard to make time to talk on the phone. Instead, my friends and I send each other voice notes. That way we can listen to them when we feel like it, and it's easier to respond by talking than it is by typing. I feel closer to people when I hear their voices too.

- **Siri/Google Home/Alexa**. Someone in my life that is willing to help me by just using my voice? Enough said. "Siri, set a reminder for..." is something I say 7 to 10 thousand times a day. I even thank her now, such is my gratitude.

- **Pay your kids to do chores**. I used to think, *Well, they are part of the family, they should just do them!* Which they did, but with a lot of subsequent nagging and carry on. I can't be bothered. I don't want to do the chores – I already do enough. You can bet your arse that I will blithely pay my kids to do them. It's not a lot per chore, just $1–$2, but if they do enough, they can get a decent amount. But they're kids, so they don't do too many. It's a win-win for me.

- **You can wash colours and whites together**. There, I said it. I will stand on this hill, and I will die on this hill. I have never separated my whites and colours, and I never will. Are my whites "brighter than bright"? No. Do I care? Also no.

I'm sure there are so many more, and I would love to hear them! In fact, I think there is another book idea right there – *Alana's Life Hacks for ADHD Legends*. Feel free to let me know if you have any you want to add. Because if there is one thing I have learned about ADHD people – we are creative.

Self-care

We make all the time in the world for other people, ensuring that their needs are met. Often, we are also advocating for our children. We are friends, sisters, mothers, daughters and colleagues. It's an easy path to slide down ungracefully as we gradually put our own needs farther and farther into the distance. It doesn't feel like a conscious decision. It feels like something that starts and snowballs until you don't even know who you are anymore.

I know that prior to my diagnosis I had completely forgotten about me. I had somehow intertwined my own identity into my children's. Because they needed me, and I wouldn't want to be anywhere else, I forgot to leave anything over for myself. The hardest part was that I didn't even know what I liked anymore.

It's quite a common trait of ADHD to have a burning desire to do *something*, but not really be able to figure out what that something is. I knew I was capable of amazing things, but my days were stretched taut, packed to the gills with stuff, and I couldn't see any way that I could claw back some of that time for myself.

Making this a priority has been one of the most difficult, but equally the single most helpful thing, I have done for myself. And my idea of what this could look like really changed. I thought I had to take up some big hobby and sacrifice other things to do it.

Turns out that, for me, it's something as simple as taking half an hour at the end of the day to crochet some granny squares. It's going for a 30-minute walk with my dogs and listening to an audio book. It's writing and filming silly videos for the internet. It's tidying the house when the kids are out and sitting in silence. It's a cliché, but you really do have to fill your own bucket.

We are getting fed this bull-dust of what self-care looks like. Apparently, if you put on a face mask and paint your toenails that should be enough to fill your bucket. My bucket must be an industrial-sized one because that kind of thing doesn't even touch the sides for me. Usually, I put on a face mask and immediately forget about it, smudging it into my eyes and getting it all over my jumper. And then I have to set a timer to remember to wash it off, but I like to ignore timers so by the time I go to wash it off it has set like concrete on my face.

Here's the secret that they don't tell you:

Self-care is being radically unapologetic about having a commitment to show up for yourself.

It doesn't matter what that commitment looks like. It must be set by you. It can change every week if it needs to. Sometimes, it is making sure I get to bed at a decent time. It's not a pretty thing I can put on my Instagram stories for others to aspire to. It might be setting up a rule that I am not allowed to go on social media once I get to bed. It's drinking enough water or making a healthy food choice when I want anything but. Other times, it's eating that KFC I've been craving.

It's not sexy or cute. It's just me showing up for myself. And here's the thing: it doesn't matter if I sometimes forget and do things differently. Self-care is also accepting yourself in all your shapes and forms. It's bucking against someone else trying to tell you that how you operate is wrong.

It's knowing that you left 437 dishes in the sink again, and that you didn't wash your hair when you really needed to, and that you haven't messaged your friend back for 39 days and still *loving yourself purposefully anyway.* You don't have to achieve a certain number of things in a day to be able to say that you're an amazing human. You are fighting something every day that has symptoms that society has told us are wrong. You're not a shit person. You're a goddam warrior.

Also, loving yourself imperfectly is fine too. You don't have to love it all, all the time. We're allowed to feel a whole range of emotions.

One huge tip I would give you is to seek out other neurodiverse people to spend time with. It's okay if these people are online friends only. We are out there, we are speaking our truth, we are finding other people who want to listen, and we want to listen back. People who take the time to really dig deep and explore why they are the way they are, and then share that with the world, are the ones doing the work. They're the ones who are showing up for all of us.

Talks too much!

Positives of ADHD

Here we are at my favourite subject.

There are SO many positives. You might not be feeling that right now and that's okay. We can't be positive all the time, and I am aware to not discount the many unique struggles that ADHD people have. However, there are also so many unique strengths that we do have.

I may be in the minority, but I am proud to be someone with ADHD. I love having a brain that thinks differently. I like that I am not neurotypical.

What happens when people lose their eyesight? Another sense, such as hearing, will compensate for their lack of vision. In an ADHD brain, the "doing things" part can be lacking, which means that the other parts of the brain have to compensate.

As people with ADHD we have endless creativity. Spend any amount of time in an ADHD support group on social media and you will see this daily. I saw someone ask for suggestions on how they could manage something they were finding difficult. Holy Batman, did these people deliver. This is a group of people, many of whom struggle with day-to-day tasks, and the level of thought people put into answering this was incredible. Finding unique ways around difficulties is not easy to do.

I also know that I have infinite amounts of creativity that I can tap into at any time. There is something so enjoyable about expressing myself creatively, and I don't just mean painting or drawing. Like many people with ADHD, I find it easy to turn my hand to most things I try. If I have an interest in something, then I can learn that subject inside and out at a decent pace.

That's because our brains are super-processors. I have a great story to back this up. When my little ADHD boy was 7, we went to the shops. As we walked towards the entrance, we saw a man walk towards a dog who was tied up there. He crouched over the dog as though he was patting it. When he saw us coming towards him, he looked surprised, stood up and walked away quickly towards his car.

I didn't think much about it, but my son said, "That man was trying to steal that dog." I shrugged this off as we entered the store. When we came back out, a well-dressed lady was untying the dog to walk home. My son's words came into my head, so I called out to the lady to ask her if she was here with a man. She said no, so I told her what we had seen.

My son piped up and said, "I saw he had a car, and I knew he wouldn't have a car and leave his dog tied up out the front. I knew he was trying to take him."

He was able to pick up and process all of that information from a split second. His observational skills picked up and translated so many things in a moment, and I was seriously impressed. He was so proud of himself, at how fast his awesome brain had worked.

There is a school of thought that back in the days of hunting and gathering, the hunters displayed tendencies of people with ADHD. Think about it – hunters needed to know how to do a little bit of everything to survive, which required flexibility and adaptability. They may have also been able to respond better to unpredictable threats and think on their feet. Hello! *We* are the reason that civilisation survived.

> ❝ *I share myself with people because sharing myself allows them to do the same.* ❞

You probably won't see it on a list of symptoms for ADHD, but in my experience – and after chatting with many other people with ADHD – oversharing can be an ADHD trait. I don't know when it was exactly that the term became a dirty word. If you look up the meaning behind oversharing, it says, *The disclosure of an inappropriate amount of detail about one's personal life.*

The use of the word "inappropriate" bothers me. Who decides what is and isn't appropriate? The definition implies that there is some overarching body who is the judge of what is and isn't acceptable. Well, guess what? There isn't. I believe the term became more common with the growth of social media. What I find odd is when people choose to follow others on social media and then accuse them of oversharing. They may have missed the memo that you can simply unfollow that person. You don't even have to say anything, you can just click the button. Ground-breaking, I know.

To me, the term "oversharing" implies that you are sharing more than another person feels comfortable hearing. And, yeah, I get it. I don't want to hear in gruesome detail about someone's surgery because that grosses me out. So, if someone starts telling me about that, I will ask them to stop. And if they don't stop – then they're a dick. Same goes for me. If I'm telling someone something, and they don't like it, then I will stop. They probably wouldn't even have to tell me because I'm observant and I can read people easily.

If you focus on the dictionary definition of the term, then you miss the good stuff that can come from oversharing. I share myself with people because sharing myself *allows them to do the same.* It is one of my greatest pleasures to watch people unfurl in front of my eyes, basking in the freedom of being their true selves. I consistently show people that I am someone they can trust and that I'm willing to trust them. I adore it when a new person I've met overshares before I can. I love that kind of freedom and willingness to buck against societal pressure to hide who you are.

ADHD people often feel the need to wear a meta-physical mask. This means we dilute ourselves so that we are more "acceptable" to neurotypical people. If you were diagnosed as an adult, then that mask might be firmly in place, to the point where you are not sure who the real you even is. The implication that the ADHD trait of over-sharing is negative is detrimental to our mental health. It's not wrong of you to share yourself. It's how you find your tribe. Using the term creates a shame story around you being you. You don't have to be ashamed of how you communicate, and the right people won't ever make you feel that way.

So many good things have come from me oversharing. If I chose not to overshare, then I wouldn't be writing this book. And, hopefully, this book is helping other women.

The moment I was diagnosed with ADHD, I fully decided to drop the mask. I used to hide how hard I found things – now I make social media videos about them so that others won't feel like they're the only ones. I get many comments from people saying how the videos have helped them to feel seen and supported. Tell me again how that's a bad thing? When I show up, unapologetically, as me, then I get to live authentically. It means that I don't have anything to hide, and I don't feel shame about who I am.

Oversharing creates connection. No one could argue that connection is a bad thing. The opposite of connection is disconnection. And disconnection leads to all sorts of problems. If more people took the time to connect, then we would be in a much better place in society.

Something else I have always been able to do is pick up on vibes. Do you find that you can walk into a social situation and instantly know when the vibe is off? Guess what? That's not your spidey senses, that's your ADHD. Our brains can process such a staggering amount of information in a teeny amount of time. This is when the inattentive label peels off and flutters to the ground.

Quite a few times this skill has worked in my favour. I was in London at a well-known club in about 2005. Spirits were high, many a drink had been taken and the place was heaving. Sweaty bodies jostled against each other in the half-light, with deep bass thumping through the speakers. I was having one of those nights where no matter how many alcoholic beverages I consumed, I was just not getting drunk. The air felt charged, like something was going to kick off at any given moment. My intuition was going into overdrive, and if I had hackles, they would have been up.

I mentioned my suspicions to a friend, who gaily shrugged them off, bopping away on the dance floor. I gazed around the room, trying to pinpoint where the feeling was coming from, when out the corner of my eye I saw a hand slip surreptitiously into a bag. A bag that was clearly not owned by them. Suddenly, I could see multiple pickpockets, sidling up to unsuspecting targets, waiting for their moment to strike. We hightailed it out of there, saved by my instinct and my skill at sensing when things are off around me.

Another positive is our compassion. Spending your whole life either knowing you are "different" or wondering why you feel different means that it's easy for us ADHD folk to feel compassion for others. We have a strong sense of social justice, and you will always find us supporting the underdog. I have noticed that my youngest son has a natural affinity for helping other people. He notices when others are struggling and will go above and beyond to help them.

At the time of writing this book, he is 7 years old. The level of understanding he bestows on people is beyond his years. His big brother developed the habit of saying, "Did I stutter?" after a sentence. If you're as old as me, then you'll recognise this as a line from the iconic movie from the '80s, *The Breakfast Club*.

My little guy pulled him up on it, saying, "That's not nice – some people do have stutters and it might hurt their feelings if they hear you say that!" He's 7 years old. What a guy.

Something else I love about having an ADHD brain is my ability to think on my feet. Let me tell you a little story about the time ADHD saved my butt. This was prior to my diagnosis but just after I started having my suspicions about ADHD.

I was at the tail end of finishing my Certificate IV in Community Services at TAFE, with four weeks to go until the course was complete. Then my lecturer dropped out. All of the people in my course were left anchorless. It was an online course, so it was crucial that we have someone to check in with, particularly with such a short amount of time until the end. Most of the written work had been done, but we still had to visit the campus to do our practical demonstrations of what we had learned. We were shunted from one person to another until finally we had some dates for the campus visits.

I arrived at one of the sessions thinking it was just a matter of me sitting down with a lecturer and discussing the module. Maybe doing some simple role-play or answering some questions. The module was about community activities – we had been asked to prepare a written plan for 3 sessions we could run for community groups. What I wasn't told was that we would be running those sessions on that day, to a group of people. The lecturer had gathered 3 other staff members to sit in, and I was in shock. To go from what was in my mind, a simple conversation, to standing up in front of all of these people, was just slightly intimidating.

What worked in my favour (and what I realise now is such a great ADHD approach), was that I'd picked 3 activities that I love – sewing, meditation and budgeting. Completely off the top of my head, I ran those 3 groups so successfully that days later, when I had a session with another lecturer, she said, "Oh, are you the one who did the sewing group? I've heard a few people talking about it!" Just call me the *Notorious ADHD*.

It doesn't end there though. I had to return the next week to carry out another practical. Again, because my lecturer was gone, I wasn't given the correct instructions. I arrived for the session and the lecturer (a different one this time) said that she trusted I'd been prepped for it and was ready to run a toolbox meeting for the Work Health and Safety module? I looked blankly at her because, no, I absolutely had not been prepped for it. For once it wasn't a case of me being unprepared – I quite literally had not been told this imperative information.

The lecturer said there was no way I could do the assessment that day because it required lengthy prepa-ration time, and I would have to come back the following week. By this point I'd been shunted around to so many different people, not given the right support and let down by the institution. Plus, I had taken a day off work to be there and didn't want to take another one. I refused to leave and asked for 45 minutes of preparation time. She wasn't impressed and cautioned that she would have to evaluate me on what I presented. No special consider-ations would be made.

Forty-five minutes later, I delivered an impeccable toolbox meeting, down to the minutest detail. I answered her questions without fault. She couldn't hide her surprise that I had actually pulled it off. And pulled it off well. I got my pass and left there on the biggest high.

Now I know that, thanks to how my brain works, I can think on my feet and come up with creative and out-of-the-box solutions. I can't remember to post a letter, but I can smash other things out of the park. If there is an emergency, then I am the person you want there. It's almost as though I've already imagined the worst-case scenario for everything, so that when it actually does happen, I'm not shocked. Something happens to my brain when there is an emergency, and my laser-sharp focus thinks of what needs to happen. I am so super aware of things happening that I'm already one step ahead.

Not only am I one step ahead, but I also have the superpower of being able to hyperfocus. If there is something an ADHD person is interested in, then you will never find a more focused person. There is no one more able to achieve amazing things than someone with ADHD who has entered hyperfocus mode. I know people who have finished half of their assignments for a course (that should have been done over a matter of months) in one night. I can get "in the zone" multiple times a day, and during this time the executive function issues I have mysteriously disappear.

> **❝ When we have the right level of interest or motivation, there is no shortage of what we can do. ❞**

When I sat down to write this book, I easily wrote 2,000 words in an hour. Considering my goal for the book was to reach 60,000 words, technically I could have finished it in 30 hours. Tell me again how I have an attention deficiency!

When we have the right level of interest, or we have the right motivation (hello, looming due date), then there is no shortage of what we can do. I know the exact activities that interest or intrigue me enough to get me into the hyperfocus zone. Some of us can inspire the hyper-fixated state by being given a challenge or being in a competitive environment. There's nothing like an impending deadline to garner a gargantuan last-minute work-fest, proving that we *can* do it, just on our own terms. The trick is to harness that and make it work to your benefit.

The only thing is, we never know if our abilities will show up when we need them. This is just one of the things about ADHD that can be confusing and frustrating. It's not guaranteed, but when you pull it off, it's magic.

On top of our ability to hyperfocus it's also common for people with ADHD to have a great sense of humour. I've spent my whole life trying to figure out how to make other people laugh. There is not much that I won't do or say for a laugh. Usually, I'll say the thing other people are thinking but don't dare bring up. I'm fully committed to looking like an idiot if it can elicit a giggle from someone. In high school I recall being moved to the front of the class, or away from a certain person, to stop me from being distracting or distracted. Like that would stop me. One time in particular, a classmate and I were in hysterical fits of giggles. He was moved to the back of the class, and I was moved to the front. I could hear him faintly snorting with laughter, and that was all I needed to be set off again.

My absolute favourite type of person is the kind who makes me laugh. I have a friend, Leonie, and sometimes I have to avoid conversations with her late at night because she makes me laugh so hysterically that I can't go to sleep. She tells this one story about a time she was turning around to point at something and instead her finger slid straight into a stranger's mouth, and she touched their back teeth. Even writing that now makes me feel the tickle of hysteria in my stomach. It's the way she tells the story too. Like, she is *horrified* by it and that makes it even funnier.

I am easily amused and easily entertained. Mainly by myself. Just this morning I had a hysterical laughing fit to the point of crying over something so silly. I was talking to my husband about a friend getting married, and I commented on the fact she had 7 bridesmaids and what I referred to as "7 brideshusbands". Just thinking about it now makes me snort, several hours later. That shit is funny.

The time I accidentally ordered the 25-cm blind, I had to actually leave my desk and hide for half an hour because I was so hysterical over it that there was no way I could deal with any customers approaching the desk.

If this is a trait of ADHD, then I'll take it. Every single day.

Talks too much!

Neuroscience behind ADHD

Let's get all science-y here for a moment and check out some ADHD facts. There are some things that I find quite interesting, and you might too. You also might not, so feel free to skip to the next chapter. But just remember that for every person who skips this chapter, a fairy dies. If you want that on your conscience, then fine.

So, it turns out that despite the people who think more discipline is the answer, ADHD is NOT a behavioural disorder. ADHD is also not a mental illness. It is also not a learning disability. ADHD is not a damaged or defective nervous system. Our nervous systems work just fine, they just work using their own set of rules.

ADHD is a developmental impairment of the brain's ability to self-manage. Although brain scientists have found that deficiencies in specific neurotransmitters underlie lots of disorders – like anxiety, mood disorders, anger-control problems and obsessive-compulsive disor-der – ADHD was the first disorder found to be the result of a deficiency of a specific neurotransmitter. In this case, the snazzy little guy called norepinephrine. Like all neu-rotransmitters, norepinephrine is synthesised within the brain. The basic building block of each norepinephrine molecule is dopa; this tiny molecule is converted into dopamine, which, in turn, produces norepinephrine.

Norepinephrine acts as both a stress hormone and a neurotransmitter (a substance that sends signals between nerve cells). It's released into the blood as a stress hormone when the brain perceives a stressful event. As a neurotransmitter in the central nervous system, norepinephrine increases alertness and interest, and speeds up someone's reaction time. Norepinephrine has been shown to play a role in a person's mood and ability to concentrate.

Dopamine is another neurotransmitter. Your body makes dopamine and then uses it as a kind of postal worker – it sends messages between cells. Dopamine is what helps control the brain's reward and pleasure centre. When someone experiences something pleasurable its levels increase. It can affect our mood, attention and movement. A healthy level of dopamine makes us feel good, helps us strive and to find things interesting.

Both norepinephrine and dopamine also help people pay attention and focus. Low levels of dopamine and/or norepinephrine can lead to the symptoms of such conditions as ... you guessed it ... ADHD. Not only was ADHD the first disorder that they figured out was the result of a deficiency in a specific neurotransmitter, but it was also the first disorder found to respond to medications to correct this deficiency. Cool, huh?

It hasn't been discovered yet whether the problem lies with a deficiency of norepinephrine itself or of its chemical constituents, dopa and dopamine. They also don't know yet exactly where in the brain the issue lies. This means that doctors have to rely on clinical experience to figure out which medication to try for each person, and at what dosage. Hopefully, there will come a time when our knowledge of the brain is much better, and the diagnosis and treatment of ADHD will be more defined.

Imagine if your psychiatrist could specifically pinpoint what and where your deficiency was.

"Alana, your ADHD is caused by a deficiency of dopa in the frontal cortex, so you need medication A," or, "Alana, you have a type of ADHD caused by a deficiency of dopamine in the limbic system, so you need medication B."

What do ADHD medications do? Basically, they raise the level of dopamine, causing the brain to synthesise more norepinephrine. Once the level is where it should be, our brains function better, and we become less hyperactive, inattentive and/or impulsive. Once the medication wears off, these levels fall again — and the symptoms return. This is why I am best avoided in the morning prior to medication and in the evening once it's worn off.

Talks too much!

ADHD things I've learned along the way

It is possible that you've read up to this point and felt as though you related to the majority of my experience. It is equally as possible that you have barely related to it at all. It's important to me to highlight the fact that many people experience ADHD in different ways to each other. ADHD exists on a spectrum and cannot be defined in just one way.

As you have heard, I am the kind of ADHD that:

- runs late
- has time blindness
- has a messy house and car
- talks a lot
- is externally calm
- overshares
- struggles to stick to routines.

However, you might be the kind of ADHD that means you are:

- always early
- chronically clean
- a lover of routines

- externally hyperactive
- quiet.

You might be a combination of both. You might change all the time. There is no one way to ADHD. And because ADHD is often experienced with co-morbid conditions, each person experiences it in their own way. Add in personal experiences, trauma, family dynamics, race, gender, sexuality and anything else you can think of – well, it's no surprise that we are all different!

Often, symptoms like being early or chronically clean can come from a trauma response. If you have spent your life being made to feel like crap for being late or messy, it's possible you've managed to train yourself to ensure that these things don't happen again. This explains why it's so important that medical professionals train specifically in ADHD because at first glance women can seem like they have it all under control. And when these women ask for help, their doctor may take a surface glance and dismiss their claims. Looking good on the surface is not an indication of what is going on inside.

Even though there can be an association between ADHD and learning difficulties, most people with ADHD have significantly higher-than-average IQs. We also use our higher IQ in a different way than neurotypical people. By the time most people with ADHD reach high school, we can find creative solutions and tackle problems that most other people can't. In fact, many people are going about their life undiagnosed because their IQ is high enough that they've been able to cover up the struggles they have. As I mentioned earlier, I didn't have any issues in school with my work. I did have slight issues with my behaviour, but it wasn't seen as bad enough to warrant thinking I needed any help.

Most adults with ADHD are not in-yer-face hyperactive. Our hyperactivity is often internal, and we don't have a shortage of attention. We pay way too much attention to *everything*. Unmedicated, I can have a squillion things going on in my mind at once. One of them is usually an annoying ear worm – you know, when you have a song stuck in your head on a loop. It's not that we have a deficit of attention, it's just that our attention is inconsistent.

I know that when I'm at work, I'm being paid to do the work I'm being paid to do. However, that is not an incentive for me. Unless the work engages me, then I struggle to focus on it and I would much rather be doing something else, like writing a book. But when I have been given a task to do, I can focus on that more than others can, and I can get that task done in half the time than others too. Or, when I realise a deadline is looming, then you've never seen someone work that fast.

Chances are you've heard of executive function. To put it plainly, anything you need to do that requires working memory, flexible thinking and self-regulation falls under the banner of executive functioning. You know, life. Traditionally, some people say that those of us with ADHD have an executive function disorder. Nope. Do not agree. We struggle to maintain our executive functioning because the world traditionally operates in a neurotypical way. I am perfectly capable of managing as well as the next person, but I need to manage in a way that suits me. I also need medication to allow me freedom from the symptoms that are debilitating.

People who have ADHD are referred to as being "neurodiverse". This term was coined by Judy Singer, a sociologist on the autism spectrum, in the late 1990s. Judy disagreed with the idea that people with autism were disabled and believed that their brains simply worked differently from other people's. This term was then applied to other neurodevelopmental conditions such as ADHD, developmental speech disorders, dyslexia, dyspraxia, dyscalculia, dysnomia, intellectual disability and Tourette syndrome, as well as schizophrenia and some mental health conditions, such as bipolarity, schizoaffective disorder, antisocial personality disorder, dissociative disorders and obsessive-compulsive disorder.

By embracing neurodiversity, we are ditching the idea that people living with autism, ADHD, dyslexia and other neurodevelopmental disorders need medical intervention to "cure" or "fix" them. Instead, we embrace the promotion of creating support systems that allow people to have an even playing field in a neurotypical world.

> *Everyone has something unique and special to offer.*

Giving people support to live their life the way that works for them is imperative. So, instead of expecting my ADHD son to sit still during class when he was younger, his teacher instead let him go outside for a run, or have fidget toys, a weighted blanket, and he was allowed extra time to finish his work. Thankfully, I was lucky enough for my son to have teachers in his early schooling who were well versed in inclusive teaching methods, and, as a result, I watched my son blossom. Not because he was behaving how he "should", but rather he was behaving in a way that showed he knew he was supported to be educated in the ways he needed to be.

Ideally, we would live in a world that extends this honouring of authentic forms of human diversity. And while there have been many inroads in this direction, with inclusion-focused services, accommodations, communication and assistive technologies, occupational training and independent living support, there is still a long way to go.

Rather than coerce or force people to adopt normative ideas of normality, or to conform to a clinical ideal, we should be meeting people where they are. This is not a burden. This is an honour. By doing this we unlock the magic inside of so many people that is hidden for much of the time. Everyone has something unique and special to offer, and they deserve the chance to offer that in a way that embraces them.

It's high time that we did. I'm going to throw out some claims here. I've seen mixed reports about the prevalence of ADHD in the world population. Some reports say it's 4 percent, others say more like 7 percent. I believe the number is actually far higher than that.

For starters, ADHD in adults is wildly misunderstood and misdiagnosed. Then we have the people who don't want to be diagnosed. That doesn't mean they don't have it, but it does mean they don't end up on any sort of record. Then there are parents who don't want to get their child diagnosed, or they can't afford to, and adults without the means to pursue a diagnosis either. Also, think about the people who don't have access to the information about what ADHD looks and feels like. Then add in a few million more who have reached an age where they wouldn't consider getting a diagnosis because it's "too late".

Personally, I think it's never too late to find out exactly who you are. Understanding myself on such a deep level has been one of the greatest joys of my life, and I could never have reached this without my diagnosis. But you don't need an official diagnosis to do this. Which leads me to how outspoken I am in my belief that you do NOT have to have an official diagnosis of ADHD to identify as having ADHD. It comes from a privileged position to be able to claim anything else.

If you are as fortunate as me and you were able to afford to have an assessment done privately, and relatively quickly, then I must assure you that you are in the minority. Then there is the hurdle of seeing a provider who is supportive. And even prior to that can be the issue of a GP agreeing to refer you to a psychiatrist. The benefit to being diagnosed by a qualified psychiatrist is that you can then be prescribed medication. There can also be a barrier with this because medication is expensive and out of some people's reach.

Saying that a self-diagnosis isn't as valid as an official diagnosis devalues many people's experience. It also implies that medication is the be-all and end-all of treatment for ADHD. And while medication is unbelievably helpful, there are so many other factors that go into someone's ability to manage their symptoms.

Just researching why your brain works in the way it does is a hugely helpful step in the right direction. Being able to self-manage and make accommodations for yourself is something that can be incredibly beneficial.

Someone once commented on one of my social media videos that videos like mine "make people think they have ADHD". Well, yeah, that's kind of the point. Although I would change the wording a little to say that my videos might make people realise that the way they've been feeling is caused by a lack of certain chemicals and neurotransmitters in their brain, and that they don't have to continue going through life without a reason for why they feel the way they do.

The person who commented on this then went on to say that basically she believed there were too many people being diagnosed, and that meant her experience with ADHD was being diluted. First of all, what the heck? Second of all, other people having ADHD doesn't dilute your experience with ADHD, it enhances it. No one owns ADHD or has more of a claim to it, and, in fact, comments like hers are dangerous. Not only do we already suffer from impostor syndrome, are less likely to put our needs first and seek a diagnosis, but many of us also have low self-esteem, and the last thing we need is yet another thing stopping us from getting help.

Self-diagnosis is not a dirty word. No one gets to tell you that your ADHD doesn't exist. I can't see a reason why someone would make up that they had ADHD – there is no benefit at all. My only thought could be that you want to be awesome, like us. In which case, come along for the ride. It's weird and messy but it's guaranteed to be interesting.

Even without an "official" diagnosis, you can still ask for reasonable accommodations at work. With a diagnosis from a psychiatrist then you should legally be able to access reasonable accommodations. Many workplaces have Disability and Inclusion plans.

Shortly after my diagnosis, my manager was an incredible help with managing my ADHD. She didn't view it as an imposition and was interested in how she could assist me to get the best out of me. We identified these issues:

- I set reminders for things and then ignore them.
- I say I understand when I don't.
- I skim-read emails and don't see whole sections.

- She replies to more than one thing in an email, and I will miss it.

The most imperative part of this was that she had the ability to remove the ego from the situation and not come at it from an ableist approach (i.e., "I'm the boss, you should do as I say," or, "You're an adult, you should just be able to do these things.") The only other people I've come across like this have been my boys' teachers, who are angels on this earth.

Together, we came to solutions that work for both of us:

- If something is urgent, she puts a post-it note on my desk. For some reason, the post-it notes activate the sense of urgency in my brain and I'm guaranteed to do the task.
- She checks that I understand. She also makes it easy to approach her afterwards if I've already said I understand when in fact I don't.
- She sends me emails only on one subject, and she highlights the most important parts.

Mainly, she is interested. She has become a safe person for me to practise my new skills as a diagnosed ADHD person. I spent my whole life pretending I was all over everything, but that was a lie. She allows me to be my true self and makes small accommodations for me to do so. I say small, but for me they are everything.

In Australia, ADHD is recognised as a disability under the *Disability Discrimination Act 1992*. This means you are legally protected against discrimination due to your disability. Most workplaces should have a discrimination policy and procedure in place; however, this is not always enough to ensure that you're given the help you need.

While it is illegal for someone to discriminate against you for having ADHD, many workplace rules are not ADHD friendly. For example, a job that requires you to be on time can be a real barrier for some people. In my jobs I have been lucky to have flexible start and finish times. If I arrive at 9:15am, then I work until 5:15pm. It's not that I'm working any fewer hours than anyone else, but instead I'm being trusted to ensure I work a full day regardless of my start time.

Rigid start and finish times infantilise people and focus on something that has no bearing on your ability to do well in a job, unless you have a job that requires you to open up for everyone else. In which case, see if that can be assigned to someone else because that sounds bloody awful.

A simple accommodation I've asked for at work is to be given deadlines. If I'm given a task with no deadline, then I just won't do that task until I get asked about it again. It just won't happen. But if someone gives me a task and asks me to have it done by the end of the week, then I will absolutely have it done by then. I might leave it until the last minute and cram a weeks' worth of effort into mere hours, but, hey, that's my superpower. The more you get to know yourself and your ADHD, the more things you can ask for.

These accommodations can help assist us in areas where we struggle. For me, it's organisation. Ugh. It's a dirty word in the ADHD world. It's not that we don't want to be organised, we do. It's just that the neurotypical way of being organised is the only system we're offered – prioritisation and time management. That doesn't work for my brain. I can't decide which thing is most important because all the options look the same. Unless, that is,

I am currently hyper-focused on that thing, and then I would choose that every time. This is how I find myself taking apart and cleaning my oven when I'm supposed to be working from home. That priority looks the same to me as the work I should be doing.

What is interesting is that there are certain things I'm really organised about. These are simple strategies I've used to make sure I don't lose certain things. For example, at one of my jobs I had an entry keycard and a key on a lanyard. It was really, really quite important that I didn't lose those guys. I made a rule to myself that I wouldn't take the lanyard off at any time, other than when I was taking it off to put straight into my work bag. I knew, without one iota of a doubt, that if I took it off anywhere else, then it was a goner. And it worked. For the whole time I worked there.

It's hard to say why that rule worked when so many of my other attempted rules haven't. I think I somehow mentally attached a level of importance to it that meant my brain was wired to never forget it. And it probably explains why I can forget to buy butter for 12 days in a row; it simply doesn't have the same level of importance in my brain.

Another thing I struggle with is routine. I honestly could not tell you how other people have and maintain routines. I can imagine there are people out there who do the exact same thing every morning. Get up, have a coffee, shower, get dressed and leave to go to work. For me, each morning is categorically different.

One morning I will wake up just before my alarm at 5:55am. I'll bounce out of bed, head down to my shed and do a 15-minute weights workout. Then I'll water the garden, make breakfast for myself and my kids. I would have made theirs and my lunches the night before (miracle), so all I would have to do is have a shower, get ready, yell at the kids 487,456 times to get ready and then off we would go at 8am. Early.

The next day I will sleep in until 7am, then scroll on my phone snoozily after a night of broken sleep. Finally, I will get up, run around like a headless chook making lunches and also decide that a full cooked breakfast is a great idea, as well as putting on a load of washing. The kids won't be able to find their shoes or clean socks. We will do the "Dance of the Late People" and leave the house at 8:37am but have to return 17 times to fetch forgotten items.

The thing is, I *know* that I have a better start to the day when I get up early, when I prepare the lunches the day before and when I make a quick breakfast. Does that mean I do any of those things regularly? No. Will I start doing them regularly? Also no. Don't get me wrong, I would *love* to remember to do them. However, morning and night are hard for similar reasons; I have either not had my medication yet, or it's worn off at the end of the day.

I could be hard on myself about these things, or I can do what I've always done and that is just accept this is how I am and roll with it. I'm a good person who is kind to people. I give back to my community, I support my friends and I care for my kids really well. I love my family, I work hard and I laugh a lot, and I'm always making other people laugh. And, yeah, I fuck up regularly, but I own it. I can't stick to things but that's okay. Instead of shaming myself for not being able to hold myself up to an unattainable ideal, I choose to love and accept myself... and take the piss out of myself on social media so that others don't feel so alone. I reckon I'm doing all right.

Finding out new things that I didn't know were ADHD related has been an eye-opener. For example, have you noticed that unless something is right in front of you, it's as though it doesn't exist? ADHD people commonly have something called lack of object permanence. For example, all those beautiful vegetables dying a slow and sludgy death in the crisper drawer of the fridge.

I'm not just referring to objects either. It can apply to people too. For years I wondered why I didn't appear to care as much as other people about some things. For example, I never really missed people who weren't there. I knew I was supposed to because I heard other people talking about their feelings on the subject. It wasn't that I didn't care about people because I did – deeply. It's just that when they were somewhere else, that's where they were.

My husband started working away 3 weeks at a time, and it was the first time that my lack of object permanence became a negative for me. Usually, it's quite handy, being that I live in another part of Australia to my family. It would be so awful if I lived in a state of constantly missing them. But when he started working away, it was like I forgot he existed.

Of course, I knew that he did exist, but my way of dealing with missing him was to unconsciously shut down that part of my emotions. It was made worse by the fact I knew he would be going away again after his weeklong break in-between swings. My brain couldn't catch up, and I felt distant. But guess what? The second he gave up working away, all those delicious feelings came back, and I was free to love him wildly. My brain is weird. But that's just how it is.

"ADHD is a trend"

I feel so passionate about this that it deserves its own chapter. It's not going to be long, but it's going to pack a punch. So strap in and come along for the ride.

As mentioned above, someone commented on one of my social media videos about ADHD and said that I was "making people think they had ADHD". She also went on to say that people like me are making ADHD a "trend". Sigh.

Here's what I have to say about that rhetoric: ADHD has been around forever. It has had different names, and it has been believed to have many different causes. What happens though (with everything) is that as we evolve, and as we have more research, we discover things we didn't know before. Then we update our understanding. Along with different names, ADHD has been shrouded by many different feelings, an overriding one of which is shame. For the longest time, ADHD was treated like a swear word, and the person with ADHD was made to feel embarrassed by their condition.

But the coolest thing started happening. We started realising that, actually, lots of ADHD traits are pretty awesome. And that the ones we struggled with could be shared, and sometimes helped. We started realising that some of the stuff we do is kinda funny, and it's cathartic to laugh at it. We realised that a lot of incredibly intelligent people have ADHD. And they started speaking up. And other people realised they felt the way these people felt too. So, they started speaking up too. And then lots of people who'd hidden and felt shame around the way they felt and behaved started to realise that maybe they didn't need to feel that way because there were people making videos about embracing their ADHD. And that perhaps they could pursue a diagnosis too.

The fantastic thing about education around ADHD is that we can recognise it earlier in our children, and we can pursue a diagnosis and help them with treatment. Early intervention is imperative for lots of reasons, mainly because helping someone, before they need to ask for help, means the person feels seen, supported and able to live their life to their best. People can experience better mental health because they're not left wondering what is "wrong" with them and why they do things so differently to everyone else around them. You see, by sharing our experiences, other people benefit.

People's understanding and knowledge of ADHD has grown. It is no longer a shameful secret but a way to understand yourself so well that you can get as much from life as someone without ADHD. It has broken down barriers and means that people feel like they can be their true selves, instead of hiding an integral part of who they are. It means that we can finally have conversations that are honest and true. And, yes, to some people that might feel like a "trend". But to people with ADHD, it feels like a breakthrough.

The end.

Not really – there is one more chapter.

Showing up anyway

There were times while I was writing this book that I was almost completely overcome by feelings of inadequacy. I hadn't been diagnosed when I started writing it, and I knew there were plenty of other people out there who knew more than me. There were so many more people who would have more tips, more ideas and more answers. Who exactly did I think I was even considering writing this book? I thought people would think that what I had to say had already been said. What if people got sick of me talking about ADHD? Who was I to stand up and tell my story? And then it came to me.

It didn't matter if anyone knew more than me. No one knew exactly what it was like to be me. What if what I have to say is helpful to someone? Should I risk standing up and taking up space? Or was it more of a risk to hide and say nothing? I had spent 39 years of my life not knowing exactly who I was. How many other women were out there who were just like me?

And just like that, I was back on track.

Women can struggle to take up their space in the world anyway. Add in ADHD, and the desire to hide is real. For years I have hidden behind jobs that are below my capabilities because a little voice told me I couldn't aim any higher than that. Like when I re-entered the workforce after absolutely kicking arse in my own business for 8 years and taking a super-easy job because I didn't know if I was able to work in the "real" world. I went from running a business with 7 employees while taking care of all the designing, planning, marketing, social media, customer service, postage, packing and just generally being awesome, to a data entry job *because I didn't think I could work in the REAL workforce.*

I am still working at the prominent Australian university as an administration assistant. This job is wonderfully secure, the work is easy and my employers are flexible. But the work itself is not in a field that I am even remotely interested in. In my time there I've felt lost and untethered, with an overwhelming feeling that I should be doing *something* with my life. I've felt like I'm lost in paperwork and boring meetings. Naturally, my reward-seeking brain has flailed around desperately trying to find something to stimulate itself.

After being diagnosed with ADHD, I tried to find an employee support program at the university. To my shock, there wasn't one. There were prominent and fantastic organisations for students. But employees living with a disability didn't seem to exist. I knew we were there, but *where were we?* As far as I could see, we needed something set up, and I was going to do it. I had a vision of a group for employees living with a disability so that we could come together and support each other.

That was about as far as I got. I needed some help. The brilliant thing about working at a university is that I work with some of the greatest minds in the world. I didn't have to look far to find the Senior Advisor of Diversity and Equity (Disability). Who, it turns out, has wanted to get something like this up and running for years, but she needed it to come from someone living with a disability. And so, the Abilities Collective was born.

Our membership has grown quickly, and the level of passion and engagement right from the start has been astounding. We get to be part of something really import-ant within the university, including having a voice on im-portant policies like the Diversity and Inclusion Plan. It's my dream for us to reduce (hopefully eradicate) stigma, education around disability and to help implement real change when it comes to inclusion and accommodation in the university.

> ❝ *We simply cannot move forward as a society if people must hide who they are.* ❞

I want people living with a disability to know they can confidently apply for roles, safe in the knowledge that they will be able to access the appropriate accommodations and that they will be walking into an inclusive and woke community. I want people to show up at work and present as their true self. I want workplaces to provide accom-modations so that everyone can work to the best of their ability in a way that works for them.

I think about what would have happened if I'd just shrunk into myself or if I'd hidden my ADHD. When I was considering whether I'd tell my employer I had ADHD, my first thought was worry that they would judge me. And this is a real concern. In Australia, a huge majority of people hide their disability for fear of judgement, fear they will be negatively impacted in their career and because of the stigma surrounding their disability. I want that to change.

We simply cannot move forward as a society if people must hide who they are.

I know this is a somewhat simplistic view. You may be thinking, *Yeah, easy for you to say*. And you might be right. It's a personal decision. But the more we speak up and take up space, the more we will increase awareness. Increasing awareness reduces stigma. Having conversations breaks down barriers.

There I was, considering whether I should tell my employer about my ADHD, then I thought about how I was open about my son's diagnosis. Almost like it was more acceptable because he "fits the mould" of what society thinks ADHD is. When I reflected, I remembered that I had told people about his diagnosis so they would know there was a reason why he needed some accommodations. I wasn't ashamed of him. So why would it be any different for me? He was brave, and I was going to be too.

And there it is – another why. I want my son to be able to apply for jobs and know that his ADHD will be viewed as a strength, not something to hide and be ashamed of. That by the time he is old enough to enter the workforce there will be so much more education and understanding that he won't have to second-guess himself or consider whether he should pretend to be someone he isn't. I am going to tell everyone about myself, too, because now I think about it, I'm proud to have ADHD. And I'm proud my son does too.

If one person reads this book and feels seen, then I consider it a success. I'm not pretending to have all the answers. We all know I don't even slightly have those. But I am showing you that you can be quite crap at what society says you should be able to do and still love the shit out of yourself. You can make promises to yourself or someone else and then forget them the next day and not be ashamed of that. You can have a messy house, or ignore reminders, or be late to everything and not be ashamed of that either.

In fact, you don't need to be ashamed of anything about yourself at all. If there is one thing I love about the world these days, it's that despite the pitfalls of social media, what we've gained is much more important. Every time I see someone showing up – imperfect, messy, flawed and real – I feel so good. Every single one of you is the perfect version of you. You can spend your whole life growing and evolving and becoming more who you want to be. It's not pretty and it can be scary but taking the steps towards loving the shit out of yourself is what this world needs. We need people like you.

Step forward. If you need help, then stand up and ask for it. And if help doesn't come, then stand up again and demand it. Help might not come in the same form as it did for me. I know that diagnosis and medication is out of reach for many, but what you can do is start the process of learning about why your brain works the way it does. And, please, if there is one thing you take from this book, it's my hope that you begin bucking against what you've always been told and just love the absolute shit out of yourself. Imperfectly perfect.

Getting to know myself as I am – free from the shackles that pinned me down for so long – has been heartbreaking, mind-blowing and fascinating. But most of all it has been liberating. Don't waste the years and years I did, feeling the way I did because I put myself last, accepting that feeling like shit is just the way it is. The greatest gift you can ever give yourself is insisting on taking up the space that is due to you.

> Be around the magic makers,
> the game changers, the world
> shakers, the light bearers.
> They will challenge you and
> uplift you. They don't play small
> with their lives.

— Michelle Cromer

References

- https://en.wikipedia.org/wiki/Neurodiversity
- https://www.additudemag.com/secrets-of-the-adhd-brain/
- https://www.ncbi.nlm.nih.gov/pmc/articles/PMC4879059/pdf/nihms-756170.pdf
- https://www.gulfbend.org/poc/view_doc.php?type=doc&id=13861
- https://www.verywellmind.com/adhd-and-imposter-syndrome-3888166
- https://adhdrollercoaster.org/adhd-medications/can-acidic-foods-affect-stimulant-medications-for-adhd/
- https://nw-adhd.com/wp-content/uploads/2017/01/ADHD-Medication-Information-Sheet.pdf
- https://www.frontiersin.org/articles/10.3389/fpsyt.2017.00170/full
- https://fertilitysolutionsne.com/blog/pregnant-one-fallopian-tube/

Printed in Great Britain
by Amazon

14718461R00138